The
EMOTIONAL
IMPRINT
of
CLUTTER

Thea Maii

ISNB # 978-0-9845118-7-7

Cover and interior design: Jim Bisakowski, BookDesign.ca

Clutter

I could write about clutter

It's all around me

I pride myself in clutter.

To me it speaks of activity

Of projects, of accomplishment

Not clutter in the negative sense

Just surfaces piled with potential

With ideas I don't want to forget or put off

I'm floating all my remnants in paper boats

On a shallow pond

Where I can see them

Dorothy Baker

The EMOTIONAL IMPRINT of CLUTTER

Table of Contents

Emotions that form clutter

To each and every client, who is in this book somewhere, I offer my deepest thanks.

To those who are still struggling and feeling overwhelmed, I offer you these words of encouragement. Use them as a candle to show you the way.

And if you are willing to take the first step by candlelight, you'll find sunlight at the end of the tunnel— then you can breathe!

Introduction

It starts off as clutter of the mind—not being able to concentrate, prioritize tasks, take advantage of opportunities, form social relationships, or move forward with life; and then it forms into piles—of paper, clothing and general mess.

At this point even small tasks become emotionally overwhelming as the debilitating mind-chatter grows, becoming a cacophony of sounds clanging and banging around in our heads. That's when you know you need help!

As we come to a better understanding of the mind-body connection, so we also begin to see that the accumulated piles correspond to emotional stagnation, leading to wrong decisions, difficulty in asserting ourselves and feelings of being overwhelmed and out of balance with the world in general.

And once the piles begin, so too, does the guilt, the guilt of knowing that we should be able to clear up our own mess but are too engulfed in self-doubt and destructive behavior to even make a start. Just how do you make a decision on what to keep and what to let go when you either want to keep it all, or want to toss the lot? Where are the boundaries?

Clutter was once thought to come from lack of time, laziness, or poor housekeeping, but now we know that it goes much deeper: it goes right back to the core of who we are, back to childhood. A pain stored in our entire being inwardly, and outwardly as mounds of clutter.

As a reformed clutterer, I know the problems well, and running my own organizing business for a number of years has enabled me to really make the connections between piles of clutter and emotional road blocks—not only for my clients but also for myself—the ones that stop us from moving forward personally and professionally and are intertwined with money, status and quality of life.

I began to see that there were many different emotional patterns connected to the piles, emotions that varied from one client to another, even though the accumulation looked the same.

For many of my clients, the first step in recognizing that clutter was a problem, was also their biggest step—calling me, a professional organizer. And for some, so I was told, this caused heart palpation, uneasiness and a desire to run.

For others, the response was guilt: "Why am I paying someone to do what I should be able to do?" When I pointed out that they were, in some cases, already paying a housekeeper, someone to take care of their kids, a personal trainer, accountant and more, the guilt usually subsided.

And occasionally, the reaction was hostility, usually from feelings of inadequacy and anger at not being able to start the clearing process themselves, although this passed as the piles dissolved, leaving them to wonder why they had resisted calling me for so long. Other clients would start the clearing before I arrived, either from shame or because they were boosted by the thought of it happening.

Feeling an emotional response of any kind should prompt us to connect the dots between the piles and the emotions, but most of us are unaware of the emotional destruction that clutter can wreak.

Just what is it about our stockpile of "stuff" that instills such hostility? Why do we have such a love/hate relationship with our possessions? Or maybe that's the point: they do possess us, consuming our time, energy and thoughts.

Fortunately for most clients, the first release was also the beginning of wanting to clear every space in their home: rooms, closets, the garage, cars—yes cars: the trunk, the inside, the dashboard and under the seats.

The open area, once revealed, was the breath of fresh air they had been looking for; finally being able to breathe comfortably in their own space, being at peace with themselves. A coming face to face with their own mind-chatter and winning—once and for all. An unexpected, and welcome, emotional release.

For sorting and organizing also clears the energy of a space, allowing the new to enter. And for many of my clients the new did arrive, in the form of increased business, promotions at work, new relationships, trips to unexpected places, and prosperity and abundance in unexpected areas.

Leave the channels open and better things will flow along. Some clients found checks, small and large, others photographs and personal items; some even found art work left by past spouses—and most acknowledged that without me being there they would have spent a couple of hours reading and going through their memorabilia, but making little progress. And that's the point. With an organizer, you keep moving because you're paying for a service. And just as you'd hire a trainer to get your body in shape, so using an organizer gets your space in shape.

But there have been many more clients who, having cleared a certain area, were content to let the rest remain cluttered. They could see a clear space and that was enough for them at that point—a small success. But in life, too, they were probably satisfied with only small successes!

Excess for some, is a security blanket; seeing a clear space as representing space in their lives, space to think, space to do. No more excuses, no more nagging chatter, no drifting around pretending to be busy, no reasons not to move forward with their lives. All emotional chatter!

And many, embarrassed at their prodigious amounts of clutter, cover the mounds with fabric in the misbegotten belief that the piles will be less noticeable. Of course, all it really does is point out that they have something to hide. If you are that ashamed of your space, then let that be the impetus to clear the mess once and for all.

Very often clutter comes from not knowing who we are, or what we want in life. If you don't know, spend time thinking of what you really want your life to be like. Many clutterers have difficulty making a decision about goals and then end up in situations they don't want to be in. So, if anything in your life isn't working, then set out to change it.

What most chronic clutterers crave, however, is not only peace of mind but also beauty, balance, simplicity and harmony. All the things they have covered over with the mountains of mess, and even though most of my clients had read all the self-help/clutter-clearing books, they still found it difficult to get themselves motivated.

But I was also surprised to find another form of clutter, one connected to those who didn't live in a cluttered space, who didn't have too much stuff and didn't need to throw anything away. These were clients who had clutter in their heads, who felt the need to be perfect, who tossed constantly but never could get down to what they thought was an acceptable number of things. The ultimate emotional clutterer.

A few, who found it easy to donate money but difficult to part with possessions, had clutter in every category, placed in every nook and cranny, as if giving things to others would somehow diminish who they were. A need to fill every space in order to feel complete. And money, being abstract, was easy to give away, while the emotional pull of possessions was just too difficult to deal with.

Beware though. Sometimes the reason for clutter is a genuine lack of space, not too much stuff, although many who have limited space often believe clutter to be the obstacle. So know what the problem is before judging yourself. If you had a larger space, would you have very little stuff—or still too much?

And, sometimes the problem isn't small clutter—papers, magazines, clothes, toys and other assorted oddments—but too much furniture for the space. If windows are partially covered by furniture, rooms will look smaller, so take a look around and see if there are pieces of furniture that you can move out. Ask yourself if you're keeping the item just to store unwanted objects, or because you genuinely like it? If you do want to keep all the furniture, then can it/they be moved to a different location?

Look at the room and see what the problem really is. Would fresh paint on the walls make the space come alive? Would changing the furniture around open up the room? Try a fresh approach and see what happens.

And remember, not everything can be donated, even if you do feel the need to find every little item a home. Sometimes things are so old, broken, or worn, that no one would want to accept them. So take a good look at what you're donating and ask yourself if you would want to be on the receiving end?

In the end, clutter is about not honoring who we are, not allowing ourselves to be authentic: and not feeling worthy and not living the life we truly want. But change the energy of the space by changing the contents, and then feel the lightness!

The Secret to being Organized

The Secret to being Organized—is to have a place for everything: whatever you take out of that space goes back after you've used it. If something else is slotted into the space, you have a floating article. Three floating articles and you have the beginning of a pile—and that's the end of being organized. If you have to remove something to get to something else behind it, then chances are that you'll start a pile.

Clearing a space requires that you make one of three decisions with regard to items.

- A definite keep.
- A definite toss.
- A maybe pile.

The maybe pile is to keep only for a few weeks. If you haven't thought of it, or dragged the item back after that time, it goes!

You may have bought a shirt because you loved the color but it doesn't go with anything else in your wardrobe. It was an impulse buy, but you're just not sure you can part with it, so into the maybe box it goes. Four weeks later you still can't match it with anything; time to move it on.

The easiest way to clear clutter initially, is to get everything you definitely know you don't want, out of your home. If you can, make a space somewhere on the ground or a clear table top, and then collect all the things you'd like to move out—big and small—into that area. Go room to room. Open up the closets, drawers, storage under the bed, bathroom cabinets, kitchen, anywhere where you store "stuff." Be objective. What do you really want to keep? What items do you really like? What clothes do you feel good in?

When you think you have everything together, then divide the items up according to where they will move to next: thrift stores, friends, religious organizations, kids' school sale, the street—for anyone who wants them—and garbage. Then, bag 'em up and move 'em out!

Once that's achieved, then you can see more clearly what's left—then the real clutter clearing can begin. If you feel overwhelmed, start small. Start to clear one area and then slowly work around the room in a circular motion. Don't jump around from room to room as it will slow the momentum. Pick a place to put all the same types of things together. Floating books collected into one place, papers, office supplies, clothes, shoes, gathered into separate areas. Collect kitchen stuff together somewhere in the kitchen until you have time to organize the entire place: bathroom, bedroom, living room, office, do the same.

It's much easier to organize all the same type of things at one time, than it is to hop around doing a few books, a few papers, a couple of pairs of shoes, maybe a few clothes.

Take the time to set up a workable system for all areas so that you don't have to constantly hunt for items.

Do the lotions and potions in the bathroom one day, books another, kitchen another.

And, finish what you start. Don't do half the job and think that you'll go back to it later—you probably won't, but you will become disheartened at not finishing.

If you have a walk in closet full of mystery stuff—and many clutterers do—pull everything out. Be brave! It's the only way to organize the things back into it—and the only way to really see what you no longer want and need. And once you've made the decision, then placing things back will take up much less time; as many of my clients learned as they saw piles of objects and clutter filling up the space outside the closet, and fearing that I'd be there until midnight putting them back!

If you find that you have only one particular type of clutter, then look at your relationship to what it is. If clothes are the problem, look at what clothes represent to you. Are you tied to an image, tied to how you think others expect you to dress?

Books, do the same. If you have books that you will never go back to read and don't use for reference purposes, then sell or donate them. If you just can't get rid of them, find out what books represent to you. Do you read books instead of socializing? Do they represent knowledge that you feel you lack? Are you afraid of being deprived of that knowledge?

Closets and Kitchen Cabinets

If things are too high and you can't reach the top of your closets and kitchen cabinets, then buy a small folding step ladder. It's wasted space if you don't use it, and if you do deposit stuff up there but can never get it down again, then it's also useless. Better to buy something to stand on and utilize the space—but keep the ladder where you most need it.

For deep shelves and cupboards, buy pull out organizers for pots and pans, tin goods and cereals, so that space isn't wasted. Use a Lazy Susan for herbs and smaller items—and use the Internet to give you more ideas.

Mail

Making time to go through the mail seems to be a problem for many, but if you sit at your desk or table with a container for recycled papers, a shredder for anything with personal information, a place for papers that need to be filed—and a place for bills that need to be paid—you should be able to get through the mail with ease. This is a one-stop system.

Clothes

There are three rules regarding clothes, and they apply to men as well as women.

- Does the garment make you look good?
- Does it make you feel great?
- Do you genuinely like it?

If the answer to any of these is "no," then out it goes. It doesn't matter if it was expensive; if you don't look or feel good in it, then it's just taking up space. Don't waste time trying to make it work, we all have clothes "we just can't get rid of" and yet we don't wear them. Bite the bullet and donate, give or toss the item.

Putting Together a Wardrobe

The same goes for your wardrobe as a whole. If you have to try on half a dozen outfits in order to find one that you like—especially when going out for a social event—then your wardrobe isn't working. Toss, donate, give to friends any piece of clothing that doesn't make you feel like a million dollars, doesn't give you confidence when you meet people, and doesn't play up your best features.

When you look in the mirror—and you must have a full length mirror—ask yourself if the color works with your skin tone, is the right shape for your body type, and does it light up your facial features? If not, out it goes.

Also, look at yourself from the back—for this you'll need to face a small hand mirror while standing with your back to the full-length one so that you can see yourself from the back.

What do you see? Clothes that wrinkle at the waist? Jackets that are too short and make your rear end look bigger? Clothes that are the wrong length and make your legs look shorter? If you are short waisted, wear longer tops to compensate so that the line doesn't break at your waist, and if you have short legs, wear slim legged pants with small heeled shoes or boots—not high heels as those accentuate a cover up! Lengthen the line, so never wear pants that are too short.

And look to see if both pant legs are the same length when you wear them. Many people have one hip higher than the other, making one pant leg shorter.

Get to know your body shape and then you'll understand what type of clothes to shop for.

If you're not sure what type of clothes to buy, then look at fashion books and magazines and choose an image that pleases you. Go to the stores and try on those types of garments. Do you like what you see? If you're not sure, then keep looking.

Better to have a few pieces in your wardrobe that you love and feel great in, than a closet full of clothes you don't really like and that force you to tug, twist or mess with them. You should go out feeling fabulous without having to "fix" your outfit during the evening. Same goes for work clothes. Clothes should give you confidence. They don't need to be expensive, just clothes that you feel represent who you are.

And don't hang onto garments that are a size 2 if you are now a size 12. You will probably never be a size 2 again, so buy new items that make you feel great for the size you are now.

If shoes are old and shabby looking and they can't be resurrected, then toss them. Shoes are often the last thing people think about, but are often the first thing others notice!

Returning Goods to the Store

Most clutterers have a pile of things to return to stores—so return them. Move them to the door and out at the first available time. If they've past their expiration date, cut your losses and donate them. If your car trunk is jam packed with returnables, take them out and sort according to stores. If the stores are all in the same vicinity, work out a route to return them—and do it all on the same day if possible.

If the returnables are Internet bought, then pack them up and mail the items or take them to a drop off center that accepts prepaid packages. The longer you wait, the less money you'll get back.

And, if you discover library books that were buried for months, or even years, take them back. It will show responsible behavior—and give you brownie points!

Usually, books that have not been returned to a library for a year or more are consider "lost" and because it benefits libraries to get the books back, they will impose a lesser fine rather than the entire amount. Check the policy of your local library and return the books.

Same for movie DVD's from rental places, send them back. You may believe that the cost of a DVD is so small that getting it back doesn't matter to the business—but it should matter to you. Be the one to do it!

Office Time

If your desk at the office is a mess, then finish a few minutes early and clear the area. It will give you more work time in the morning if you come into a clean workspace, as opposed to one that immediately clouds your mind. At home, put aside a couple of hours each week to organize papers, hang up clothes, pay bills and anything else that needs clearing. Make it a habit by doing it the same time each week, maybe Sunday morning, even if you have to get up a little earlier to do it. If you're a night person, do it at night.

As an Organizer, I found that four hours was the amount of time that people could deal with clearing and filing papers, after that their minds fogged over and they were screaming for relief!

Papers, for most of us, are about taking a necessary action; often to pay a bill, write a letter, make a phone call, check a bank balance, or send a check to an organization—all representing skills that most of us we were never brought up to do—and many of them connected to money, guilt and authority.

If you get into the habit of clearing the papers once a week, a four hour filing session won't occur.

And remember, the place where you work is not a place to keep everything you don't want cluttering your space at home. It is not a place to keep personal papers, bills to pay, or anything with personal information. Most people have no idea who comes into their office to clean, deliver, or snoop—after they've left for the day.

E-mails, when and how to deal with them, are a problem for many people as they take time away from other equally important jobs. But if you see them as part of your work, not as an intrusion on your time, then you're more likely to set time aside to go through them.

Delete the junk mail first, that way you can really focus on the rest, then go down the list to find the most important ones. Take action on those first, then answer the others later in the day. And don't get caught into sending long garbled e-mails that only require a simple note. Clutter clearing also applies to the letting go of unnecessary words and to simplifying thoughts.

If you choose to go through e-mails in the early morning, do them before or after breakfast. E-mails often bring up all kinds of emotions—and take time away from eating good nutritious meals—so better to enjoy the meal first, then tackle the aggravation!

Storage Spaces

Do not pay for a storage space outside the home, unless it's imperative. Ask yourself why you feel the need to have one. Are you parking furniture from family—usually from parents who have passed on—just in case you will use it later, or the kids may want it, later? Use it now or find a home for it, or, if it is worth money, sell it.

And, if you're saving empty boxes from all the appliances that you've bought over the years, then ask yourself if you will ever send back for repair, a five year old toaster?

Sort out which boxes you really do need to keep and then recycle the rest.

And If you've just moved into a new space and have all the boxes broken down, list them on a web site and let others collect and use them. A good deed, and a good use.

Memorabilia and Special Things

Take one medium size box, plastic of cardboard, and use that box only for memorabilia. Most items saved are small: T-shirts from college, school year book, school reports, medals and trophies, items from trips and other meaningful things collected along the way. Photographs—which are usually numerous—are better saved in separate cardboard boxes.

And if you have clothes, jewelry and other things that you are keeping for special occasions, know that those times are few and far between. Better to wear those things when you want to feel special—without needing permission.

Treasures that have been handed down usually remain precious to successive generations—meaning, that no one dares to wear or use them.

Be the one to change that!

Cables and Small Things

Use zip lock bags of varying sizes. Use them in the bathroom, office and kids' rooms. They allow you to see what's inside while keeping small items and cables wrapped.

Go through your cables and appliances and see what matches. If you don't have the appliance for the cable, dispose of it.

Family and Friends

A word of warning about family and friends helping you to clear your mess: Don't let them! They may be well-meaning, but they already know you have a problem and at some point it will come back to haunt you. Either that, or you'll get bogged down within the first few minutes looking at your stuff, and little will be accomplished. If they keep volunteering their time to help you, they're really sending you a message that you're place is a mess and they think you're incapable of clearing it on your own. Surprise them by getting the space cleared and then invite them over. End of story!

Housekeepers and cleaning people

If the people you hire are shoving things behind cupboards and in any available space, then not only do you have an organization problem but you are paying someone to complicate your life, forcing you to spend hours searching for things you may never find.

If you don't have a system, then how can they follow one!

And maybe what you really need isn't a cleaning person but a housekeeper.

What's the difference you say? Well cleaning people clean—many actually taking pleasure in their work—but housekeepers do, and should do, more. Housekeepers shop, keep the kitchen stocked with food staples, take out and pick up dry-cleaning, and do small jobs that relate to the running of a home. And they know where everything should go.

When you add up the time spent doing all the small jobs, and compare it to paying someone else to do them for you, it often becomes more cost-efficient to pay a housekeep a few dollars more per hour, than to pay cleaning people who can increase organizational problems.

Travel

Most of us only think about travel when preparing for a trip, but taking action beforehand can save a lot of time and angst.

If you are leaving the country, find your passport ahead of time—it may have expired! And check the visa and inoculation requirements of that country too.

Things that you use only for travel—hand steamer for clothes, plug adapter, clothes line and clips, nylon bags to pack small garments, plastic bags for oddments you may want to bring home—keep inside the suitcase, even when not in use, that way you won't have to hunt for them before the trip.

Write out two lists; one to go into the suitcase, the other into the bag for toiletries. For the suitcase, list all the things that you use on a daily basis but don't usually think about; eyeglasses, inner soles for shoes, charger for the phone, other important items. Write them down as you think about them.

Do the same for the toiletries. List everything you use in a week/month at home—hair dryer, creams, razor, toothpaste—and then keep the list in that specific bag—at all times.

If you keep the list in the appropriate place, everything you need for the trip will be covered, and everything you need to pack when returning home will also be packed—meaning no items left at the hotel!

- Pack small items in zip-lock bags—scarves, first aid things, maps and travel information, anything that requires keeping a number of things together.

- Small pieces of jewelry, place in plastic, travel pill boxes—they close firmly and won't get lost in your purse.

- For larger pieces of jewelry, use eyeglass cases. If you don't wear eyeglasses, buy the cases—or find a friend who wears glasses and doesn't know what to do with them all. Perfect for protecting jewelry when traveling, and from thieves—who would open an eyeglass case!

And don't over pack. Ask yourself how many trips you've taken in the past where you packed clothes, only to bring them home again unworn. Now that airlines are tightening up their policies—and making new ones—about the amount of luggage allowed, lighten your load. In most parts of the world you can buy the basics necessities, but if you are taking a trip to some remote part, check what they sell—and what you can purchase—before taking the trip.

For things that you can't pack ahead—medications, makeup, baby bottles—make a list and leave it in a prominent place—to see before taking the trip!

If you have the space, a spare room or an unused area, then open up the suitcase(s) a few days or weeks ahead of time, then when you think of something you want to take, put it in. Yes, you will have to repack, but you will also have everything that you want to wear and use at your destination. This is especially useful when packing for a family trip which often becomes a last minute rush, when everyone is frazzled and can't think clearly.

If you are traveling with small children, pack a surprise package. It's amazing how quiet small children can be at airports, in cars and trains, when given a new toy. Most parents pack their child's favorite toy(s), but don't think to buy new ones to ease the tedium of waiting at airports. It will also keep the child awake until you get onto the plane, which is where, hopefully, they will fall asleep.

Make your next trip something to enjoy, not something that will give you sleepless nights.

Clutter and Time

Clutter is the monkey on your shoulder constantly reminding you of your own mess.

You walk halfway across a room and something grabs your attention, then something else, then another, and so it goes, and before long, two hours has gone by but none of the clutter. You make coffee, read the paper, pick up a magazine, make phone calls, e-mail friends, all distractions and all interrupting the clearing process.

If you have the resolve to clear the clutter on your own, more power to you. Do it!

Don't talk about it as something you're going to do. Just do it. And then show everyone that it's done. The reason for hiring an outsider, however, is that she/he has no emotional connection to your possessions, unlike you, who are joined at the hip to everything you have—even junk mail! Allow the energy of your place to change and increase prosperity, let new relationships come into your life, new opportunities, new jobs, a change of residence.

Let the old go - embrace the new!

The Magic Threes

If all else fails, apply the Magic Three formula—and feel like a winner.

- Pick three items of clothing each week to make a decision on - keep, toss, donate.

- Pick three files each week from your filing cabinets filled with old files and go through them—recycle, shred, rename or start a new file.

- Pick three items from your kitchen cabinets and decide what to do with them. Often people store broken, old or unused items in cupboards that could be better used.

- Fill three supermarket bags of things to donate and then get them out the door. Don't wait until you have filled whole boxes.

- Got three strollers for one child? Y-es, it does happen, and all too often, unfortunately. Pick one and donate or sell the other two. And best of all, get the child walking as soon as possible, which will increase curiosity and creativity and save on medical bills later in life.

- Got three bikes per person? Do the same.

- In fact the Three principle can be applied to almost anything, and three here and three there all add up over time.

■ And one more thing about the Magic Threes: I've found that it usually takes three times before most clutterers are really willing to let things go. This entails three organizing sessions spaced a couple of months apart. The first time, clients are willing to part with only a small amount of items; things they really don't like or want. The second time they are willing to toss much more. The third time, they are really able to release a large amount of items, things they no longer wear, use, read, or like.

Tips for hiring an Organizer

- The organizer should be nonjudgmental. This is very important. You don't need your mother making comments!

- After talking with you, she/he should know where the best place is to start, even if it isn't the place you think needs clearing first.

- She/he needs to be a good listener. Getting organized is like going to a shrink: all the emotions bubble to the top.

- She/he should be sufficiently clued into you to know when to back down, be able to work around issues, and not be combative.

- The organizer should want, and like, to organize. This is very important. They should not be wannabe Interior Designers using organizing as a way to move into design! Nor should they talk you into buying expensive replacements for things you already possess—bookshelves, large containers, file drawers, plastic boxes and other useful things. They are there to help you to downsize your clutter—and move out any boxes, baskets and other small containers that you no longer need.

- If you do hire an organizer, be realistic about how much you will be able to clear in one session. If the clutter has accumulated over a number of years, it's not going to disappear in a matter of hours.

- And lastly, it is very important for you to make the decision on what to keep and what to move on. If someone else makes the decision for you, then things will be tossed that you may have wanted, which will lead back to the mind-chatter rearing its ugly head again as you look for objects that you can't find, or, items that you wish you hadn't been talked into giving away.

- If you are not in control of the process, and the chatter starts—this time connected to clutter that has gone—it could last a lifetime as you obsess over lost items!

How to use this book

- Skim the Table of Contents.

- Pick out the headings that you think pertain to you, the ones that relate to who you are and why you clutter.

- Read these sections. Then read the ones you think MIGHT apply to you. In all probability, you won't fit neatly into just one area.

- If you still haven't found the ones that seem to explain why you clutter, then read through them all. At some point something will strike a chord, and that will start the process of remembering—and the questions. And once the questions start, so the answers will begin to clarify too.

- Knowing why you clutter is half the battle and will then help you to clear, and keep, the clutter under control.

If you're giving this book to someone you know, remember that many people who clutter live their lives in denial, so don't expect miracles. The best you can do is to give them the book and hope that at some point curiosity will get the better of them and they will then take the initiative.

Starting the clearing process is an indication that you want better things in your life and are ready to move towards them. As an organizer, I found that I would often get the phone calls from people wanting to start NOW. After months of waiting, they had finally reached the point of being able to let go—of the past, old relationships, marriages and other emotional ties. They had also accepted the present—warts and all!

Emotions that cause clutter and how to clear them.

1

Getting even with Parents.

As strange as it may seem, many people who accumulate piles everywhere and who can't part with anything, are often angry at their parents for real—or perceived—hurts.

"Why did you abandon me?"

"Why didn't you support me, emotionally or economically?"

"Why didn't you have time for me?"

The need to blame comes from being hurt as a child, and as a way of getting back at the parent(s) it becomes a physical block that stops the flow of positive energy into their own souls and spaces. Over time this distress grows into a self-destructive streak that blocks forward movement and turns inwards to stop any kind of pleasurable activity.

"I'm not going to become a success and I'm going to make you feel guilty for my situation" is the unsaid implication. And wallowing in self-pity they persist in the belief that if they'd been given more support they could have made it, although the type of desired support runs the gamut: physical, emotional, economic, a better education, anything that they perceive has brought them down, and not up. These clutterers have a book full of excuses all framing themselves as the victim, and the parents as the problem.

We all suffer from this "disease" of blaming parents in one way or another, and it appears in many guises. For some it becomes the push needed to succeed in life, but for many more it turns inwards into self-destructive behavior and piles of clutter.

"I'll live in a pigsty if only to get even with them" is the thought that runs through the heads of these clutterers, even if their underlying personality values being well organized and craves a clean, spacious place to live with all the comforts and pleasures of life.

How dare their parents, who supposedly have brought them down, live happy lives, while they are floundering around in chaos? Why should they make their parents proud and happy?

The same thinking also extend outwards to family, friends and coworkers, many of whom are well meaning and have offered help to clear the clutter on numerous occasions.

Some, even move into economic difficulty, plunging them deep into debt in order to stay poor and realize their own self-fulfilling prophecy of not being able to make it on their own. And by denying themselves an acceptable place to live, they also deny the social connections that go with a clean, inviting home, eventually moving them down the social ladder, not up. As the same destructive behavior continues at work, with messy work habits and chaotic paper piles, many get demoted, or even fired from their jobs.

Living in squalor is a way to keep their parents guilt-ridden and make them pay the price, and so clutter clearing, for these people, is out of the question!

The Remedy

Of course, this kind of clutter problem harms the clutterer more than the parents, and in all probability, neither parent is really aware of the hurt, or would know how it originated even if they were confronted. If you do remember where the hurt came from then you have a head start on finding the remedy, although clutter is not usually the only indication that all is not well.

If on reading this, however, it strikes a cord, hits a nerve, or gives you a headache, then you'll know this is where the clutter issue originates. So drop the bitterness, even if you have to pay an organizer, and move forwards to better things. We all drag painful memories along, and over the years the baggage just gets heavier and heavier, slowing down our lives until we come to a stop—represented by the piles of clutter. Then we wallow in self pity and excuses about why we can't get organized.

> **SUGGESTION**
>
> If talking to your parent(s) is too difficult, then write them a letter: letters give people time to sit and digest the content. If they then wants to talk things over, give them the opportunity. Each generation blames the one before, sometimes the blame is valid, other times, misplaced, but listening to both sides will clear the air – and you may even find that both persons' recollections of the event(s) are a little distorted.

The only way out of this situation is to make peace with it. If you can trace the distress back to something tangible, then confront your parents with it; but be prepared for resistance. Most likely, they won't even remember the situation that you've been dragging with you for years, and even if they do remember it, they will have a different recollection of the events than you have.

If your parents are open to discussion, sit down with them, but if not, find other ways to accept the situation. Read self-help books on dependancy. Take anger management classes. Get out and become more social and talk to others. Talking to others is a great way of minimizing your own hurt, especially when you realize that others have the same kinds of wounds connected to their childhood.

Try to understand what the piles of clothes, papers and general mess represent. Was your home neat and orderly, a clean home—and the time spent keeping it clean seen as being more important than time spent doing fun things with you?

Did your father always have to deal with the bills and papers—before spending time with you? Did you feel deprived of time, playtime, love?

Did your parents want you to believe that the family was wealthier than they really were, keeping money worries from you, but which then gave you a false sense of how much money was actually available for the things you wanted? Or, were you ashamed of your home?

Your parents, in all likelihood, did the best they could for you given what little information they had. Each generation tries to open the communication channels a little more than the generation before them, trying to steer their kids through life without the bruises they encountered. And some do a better job of this than others.

Most hurts that appear in childhood are often small things that become big to the child.

So get going and clear the clutter—along with the memories—and stop hurting yourself.

Live in the kind of space you'd really like to live in. Success, after all, is the best revenge!

2

Successful Mothers - and Fathers.

This is a different issue than just wanting to get even with parents since it connects to self-worth, status and attractiveness. I was witness to clients with this clutter problem numerous times, but more so with daughters who had successful mothers than with males who had successful fathers; although sons did seem to have greater addictions to drugs and alcohol than the daughters.

Many have been so worn down by having successful, gregarious parents that they eventually feel they don't deserve a place in society, and certainly not a place of success. They learned as children to step back and be invisible, while the adults stepped forwards to be "the life and soul of the party." A hard act to follow at any age.

It isn't that the successful mothers and fathers want shrinking violets for children; quite the contrary, most would love to have gorgeous, talented, outgoing, successful kids— carbon copies of themselves, children to show off so they can compete with other parents and their wonderful offspring. The word here of course, is "compete"—in all arenas—and these kids quickly learn that they are just not cut out to be competitive and don't want to have to do pony tricks to be accepted. With this in mind, they then start to shrink from the spotlight. Children of celebrities and other successful parents often hit this minefield, especially as they get older.

These kids learn from an early age to blend into the background; becoming wallflowers and not orchids. The message received when they are very young, subconsciously or otherwise, is "Don't compete with me," which makes it a double whammy for the child who is often an underachiever and not so hot in the looks department. Many also become overweight as a way of building a wall around themselves, usually to keep parents from getting too close with their hurtful words and criticism.

But, most of all, they want to be noticed for who they are and not objects of desire or envy; to stand up and say, "I'm here and I'm important too," without having to constantly be on show or competing for attention against a lot of other pushed children.

As the years go by these young people often become less and less attractive, and if they do happen to be born attractive, will make themselves as unattractive as possible with drink, drugs and unfavorable friends. These kids are conflicted throughout their lives, with one foot in the world of success and the other in the world of plain, plodding and mediocre. For those lucky enough to stay in the background and make it through, they often make peace with their status, vowing to become better parents than their own, with home and family becoming more important than chic, trendy and happening.

Unfortunately, for many more, cluttered spaces represent feelings of unworthiness; not just regret at their own shortcomings but also in the form of guilt of not having lived up to their parents' expectations.

They haven't achieved enough to deserve a clear, open place to live.

The Remedy

Understand that as a human being, you breath the same amount of air, take up the same amount of space—and at census time, you too are counted. Come out from the shadows and dress like you mean it. Start with a new hairstyle or wear something that you don't normally wear. Listen to what your friends suggest. They may see the hidden you trying to escape—even if you don't!

Know that your opinion counts, so don't back down in conversations, practice with friends if you need to. No one likes rejection, but see how liberating it feels to win, even in small ways. Or, if you are good academically and the parent is not, then go for the big time and head towards a Ph.D.

Imagine how much better your mother/father would feel if you were to become a success; an even bigger success than they are. Yes, they would feel threatened at first, but imagine how much closer you'd be with them if you had more things in common, if you were able to talk about social events, sports, business, or just to introduce them to your world and your interests. If you were able to find some common ground to hold a conversation, without lowering your standards in order to shame them. To be able to understand more clearly why they feel the need to be flamboyant and constantly on display. To drop your wounds for a while, in order to see their hidden hurts.

Ask yourself how much of your clutter is attributable to lack of self-worth, and how much of it exists to make your mother/father feel guilty for your situation. Is the clutter really directed at them—or yourself?

SUGGESTION

Make an effort to see your parent(s) in a more positive way, and think how fortunate you are to have such interesting family members. See their vibrancy as a light in the world – but know that you hold the switch to their light bulbs!
Go to a hardware store and buy a light switch, and place it somewhere in your home as a daily reminder of that fact.

Closing yourself down into a small space with little room to maneuver, is linked to closing down career opportunities too, so spread your wings in space and let your career fly.

Instead of seeing the parent in a negative way, think how fortunate you are to have such interesting family members, even if you have little interest in following in their footsteps. See their vibrancy as a light in the world—to be taken in very small doses.

It should be noted, that many of these parents secretly feel guilty for the situation their kids end up in, but would never attribute it to themselves even when confronted with the overwhelming truth: the show must go on at all costs.

So you may never be the life and soul of the party, but maybe you don't need to be.

Find something that's yours and be a success at it—even if it's a hobby. Your parent is looking for small things to be proud of, so start small and build. Along the way you might actually find something big and important that you are really good at. Grasp it and know that you can be the star, and that it's okay for you to take center stage.

And if the parent still feels threatened, then move on to friends who will support you and not criticize every little word, action, or look.

3

Not feeling worthy of a nice home

Most of us don't feel worthy of much, but that comes from living in a hierarchical society which is constantly telling us that in order to be somebody, you have to have letters added before or after your name, or be wealthy, influential, attractive, and/or talented. Unfortunately, working in the arts and being creative doesn't count, which rules out many compulsive clutterers! But it's hard to feel important against these odds.

Feeling worthy comes from a belief that you have something significant to contribute to society, but that contribution has usually been defined by someone else and by their values—not yours.

We live in a society where our worth is constantly being undervalued—or even worse—that we have undervalued ourselves, and we define ourselves by those around us; often starting before we enter school and continuing on throughout our lives. Childhood determines which criteria we will use to define that worth, with money usually heading the list. And living in a youth culture that states, usually through the media, that we should have made millions by our twenties, and if not then we must be a failure, only compounds the distortion about money and success.

More surprising though, is that having too much money can affect people in negative ways just as much as having too little. And those with money handed down to them often end up with just as much clutter as those without money—it's just more expensive clutter.

And many who have come from a moneyed background will often buy expensive things to compensate for lack of self-drive, feeling that if they can buy enough "stuff" it will deaden the pain of having no goals, aims or career path: visible signs of affluence taking the place of achievement.

These people build piles slowly, often acquiring other spaces, as they leave possessions with friends, pay for extra storage, and even require an extra house or apartment for storage, but seldom go back to these possessions—and would never consider downsizing.

These are the clutterers who don't want to come home. Don't like being at home. Don't see their space as home. They work late, play late, stay with friends, anything to not have to deal with the reality of an empty life.

On the other hand, many who have made their own money also end up as clutterers by wanting to show by accepted outward objects of wealth, that they have arrived. These are people with just too much money and too little self-confidence, and they fill their homes—often with bad taste—as a way of constantly reminding others, and themselves, that they have in fact, made it.

Feeling unworthy and being surrounded by clutter can also produce feelings of being on a camping trip, a transitory situation that negates having a nice home.

The Remedy

Contributing to society doesn't always have to mean contributing money, and building a self-image on economic value discounts any regard for the relationship to the value of your time, so why not volunteer instead. Teach kids to read; help in soup kitchens; be supportive of friends; give time to listen to those who feel silenced; write letters in protest; join marches and stand up for those who are discounted: contributions to mankind that are all valuable.

If you have built a wall of clutter in your life in order to make you feel lousy, then obviously you've succeeded! But wouldn't you rather have a great home where you can invite friends over and relax: no pressure, no competition, no need to constantly feel "on?"

Feeling worthy of a well organized, comfortable space, also comes from feeling calm and fulfilled in that space. Feeling that you have room enough to breathe and that you deserve to be in it,

---

SUGGESTION

Buy a small notice board and place it where you will see it daily. Cut out pictures and photographs from magazines of all the things you'd really like in your life – clothes, home, things to go into the home, places you'd like to visit – and then stick them all on the board. Look at this at least once a day, telling yourself that you do deserve good things in your life. If your dreams and goals change, then change the pictures accordingly, but aim high!

---

shutting down the mind-chatter to just enjoy the space, as space.

If feeling ashamed moves you from one cheap, unacceptable space to another, while looking through the window at others who are moving up, then resentment will build—along with more clutter to fill the emotional void. And society is filled with images that lower our self-esteem—overweight people are thought of as being less. Tall men earn more then short men. Not having the right car, gorgeous husband/wife/kids, homes filled with the right TV, computer, stereo system, appliances or decor, all chip away at our psyche.

Not having an attractive space also prevents us from building a nest, so stuff just keeps on growing in the hopes of building one.

On the other hand, many people who do grow up in fabulous homes feel as unworthy as others who don't, so the space is not the problem. What the space represents, is.

Was your childhood home a showcase; a perfect home to show off to others? Or filled with a mess that represented a family of which you were, and are, ashamed? At what point in your childhood did you get the feeling that you didn't deserve a great place to live? Or, are you afraid you might end up just like you're parents; in a nice home, filled with nice things, in a nice neighborhood—and hating every minute of it?

Did anyone tell you how great you were? That you had an opinion of value? That you could be a success—and be compensated accordingly?

Usually, there is one sibling in each family who outshines the others and they become the bench mark for the rest, but what if the others don't want to become lawyers? If family disapproval grows based on the level of your clutter, then cut the cord and build a network of friends who will be supportive, and make you feel good about yourself. Don't try to compete for attention at family gatherings— accept that you may never be the favorite son. Instead, work on your own life, career, projects, goals, and become a success at that.

4

Fear of Success

Sounds ridiculous; everyone wants to be
a success—right? Wrong!

Success, like money, brings responsibility and many people are afraid of responsibility.

The mind games usually start with, "I'm not qualified/ mature enough to deal with this." "I'm not good enough" or "I know I'll screw up."

As the mind-chatter grows, so too, do the excuses—and the clutter. They blame lack of time, too much to do, too many hassles to deal with, too much of everything it seems, except the desire to succeed. But if you ask these people if they do want to be a success, most would answer with a resounding "yes." They just want it given to them without the baggage.

Clutter takes time and energy and most chronic clutterers will tell you that they don't have enough hours in a day to deal with everything. What they don't tell you is that they can pick up one piece of paper from the pile and obsess over it for the next couple of hours.

These people are often afraid of moving forwards, of not being good enough, not being perfect. They have difficulty making a decision about what to do with all the mess, just in case they make the wrong decision, and they live by the "what happens if........." scenario.

Having piles of clothing, papers and general mess is a great excuse for these people to avoid reality; of having to do the work, of taking the falls, taking the criticism, and a belief that "If I don't put myself out there, I can't get hurt." When they don't progress in life, however, these clutterers never understand why, all they know is that they do want to be a success, life just doesn't seem to play fair.

Many blame parents for the road blocks in their lives, blocks that have led to their failure, their lack of success. And as a way of getting back at the the parents, guilt is used to make them pay—usually in the form of real money—while others make the excuse that successful people are just lucky, or helped: helped by those they don't have access to.

Some think of success as being selfish. They look at successful people and find fault in their character—and they don't want to be like that? Better to be unsuccessful and nice, liked, accepted, bland. This pertains especially to women, and is reinforced by the media, parents and coworkers.

Nice girls finish—just usually last!

Many more feel that success will change them, change the balance of friendships, or even lose friendships, lose that security of having people around who know them well.

Success to these people represents too much of everything and they would rather devote their time and energy to the success of others, playing the martyr game to perfection.

And yet there is a certain validity in all the excuses. Helping others out, working overtime, helping at all those functions, volunteering; all require time and responsibility, probably, much more responsibility than they would have by being successful in their own right.

But clearing their homes and giving themselves free time would change too many balances in their lives.

The Remedy

Success can be sweet, rewarding and inclusive—as many have found. It can also be the best self-confidence booster, as many others have discovered. It shows that you didn't take their word for it when they told you you'd never make anything of yourself; never would become known, were wasting your time practicing, would never make money.

Success can be a role model for children, giving them a chance to do well at whatever they put their minds to, while it also tells parents they did do a good job and that all the hard work was worth it.

Delve back to the messages you received growing up. What did you hear about money? About the rich not being nice? That money won't make you happy? That money doesn't grow on

> **SUGGESTION**
>
> If your life/job doesn't connect you to successful people, and growing up you didn't meet them, then go to places where successful people often go. Become a volunteer in a well-established organization, soup kitchen or thrift store. Many successful people volunteer their time, so find out where they are volunteering and join them. See success in action.

trees? Or maybe the words were missing, but your parents' actions spoke louder than words.

Tell yourself that you do deserve to be a success. That money doesn't have to be bad. That good people can also be rich. That money can do good in the world, and that being poor accomplishes little—except adding to world misery. And money can give you a much more powerful voice when fighting for the rights of others.

But best of all, success brings money that opens doors and allows you to do good for those who need it. It's hard to be charitable in thought or deed, if you're struggling too!

Practice taking more responsibility at home and work. Read books on the lives of successful people, and be inspired to take more risks. Be more productive and use time wisely, but don't spend your time in office gossip, which is the antithesis of success. Success can be intimidating and threatening if you are moving up, while they are not, leading to excuses for their inability to move forwards, while putting your success down to luck, opportunity, nepotism—indicating that they don't have access to those things.

If you were born into a successful family where you were given everything, then the drive to succeed and accomplish an objective is often difficult—something many wealthy parents don't grasp until they have a child on their hands with no aims or goals. Growing up in a successful family can dull the flow of creative and inspired thinking, and the push to put those ideas into action.

If you are carrying resentment as a response to your family's achievements, then know that you also carry a successful mind waiting to emerge—if you'll just give it a chance.

If your parents have flattened your enthusiasm, distance yourself until you achieve something that YOU are proud of. Many parents, who never fulfilled their own potential, try to protect their offspring against the hard knocks in life by not being too positive about their child's potential. If you harbor anger at your parents for their perceived lack of drive, change the mind-chatter and stop being self-destructive—which ultimately is against you, not them. Start to clear the clutter that is stopping the flow of creativity, and a better life.

5

Fear of not having enough

The biggest fear for those who are afraid of not having enough, is that if they let something go, nothing will come in to fill that void.

Fear of shortage forces these people to hoard, to clasp things dearly to them, especially family and friends, letting go of nothing: possessions, people, past incidents and hurts.

These clutterers like living in the past and no one is going to drag them out of it. No one!

They live in the past as if the present didn't exist, and everything in their home is a testament to that mindset.

It's all about what was, not what could be. There are no possibilities, no future; only the past. A past that, for them, has been unkind and uncaring.

The fear of shortage pushes these people to the head of the line—whether they deserve to be there or not—in stores, restaurants, anywhere where others are waiting their turn.

The EMOTIONAL IMPRINT of CLUTTER

They buy more than they need and have closets and cup-boards full of food, paper goods and other assorted items, just in case. The bathroom is filled with half-used bottles and dated pharmaceutical drugs, because they may need them at a later date, even though the later date has already expired. And the closets are bulging, even though many of the clothes no longer fit.

Fear of not having enough also, and especially, extends to love, and often the children of these clutterers are not allowed to leave, and if they leave physically, are never allowed to leave emotionally. Daily phone calls from the parent keep them in line, and if the right response is not forthcoming, then illness is feigned. "I'm having a heart attack." "I'm having trouble breathing." And if the children do escape, then the ultimate guilt button is pushed—"No one cares about me!"

If the kids or other family members do try to clear up the mess, their offers are refused. If the clutter is cleared, there are no more excuses to call the the family to order. No rallying call for them to rush over as another disaster unfolds. These clutterers need a calamity in order to feel important, and so, the clutter must stay, gaining in strength daily while all those around leave—the very thing the clutterer fears the most, being left alone.

Clutter for these people is a form of mind-control, some-times unconscious, sometimes not, but games played out constantly, with past lovers, husbands, wives, kids, family members. Photographs are kept, as are letters and other incriminating pieces of evidence. Evidence of a wrong done against them many years ago, so nothing can, or, must be thrown away.

Many of these people lack self-confidence, especially when it comes to making decisions, and have spent so long relying on others that they no longer know how to make clear, unemotional decisions that could reduce the mess—or improve their lives.

But the clutter is now more important than moving on to something better, so the clutter must remain.

The Remedy

Fear is the overriding emotion connected to lack, and fear is connected to the adrenals, fight or flight. It is also linked to self-confidence and the ability to make good judgments—in this case decisions connected to clutter: what to keep and what to discard.

If you hoard everything for fear of making a bad decision, then trust your judgment a little more. What's the worst thing that could happen if you did throw something out?

Did your parents constantly belittle you about decisions you made, so believing them, you now belittle yourself?

Rethink your position on who you are and your connection to all the items that form the clutter—barricades

---

SUGGESTION

If you don't already have a savings account, start one. If you do already have one, start a separate savings account for a special project, trip or splurge. Put aside a certain amount of money each week – something that you can afford – and keep building the account until you have enough for your plan. Then, enjoy without guilt – or the fear of not having enough.

that have now formed to keep you in and your loved ones out. Items that hold all your hurts, disappointments, heartaches and control.

Time to let all those negative emotions go, along with many of the items that have formed the cluttered mess. Move them out and let others have the joy of them.

If you were given gifts as a child and they came with strings attached—obligations to be paid back at a later date—then remember that you're no longer that child. You are now an adult who can let the control go that others held over you, or, you can now become the controlling one over others, especially those you love. Which do you choose?

Think of the letting go of the old as an entry point for the new.

Let your family go. Children and other family members are far more likely to come back to you if you let them come of their own free will—not from guilt. Enjoy their company when they are with you and take an interest in what they're doing. Give them something you treasure to show how much you appreciate them, and let the gift go without strings.

Try letting one item out of your life each day, then see how that feels. Don't phone your kids—for just one day. See if they call you? If they don't, let it go. Learn to trust them more, and the phone less. And if the family want to help organize your mess, let them. Be positive and let them help you to make a decision about the item. See it as a clearing process for the body, mind and spirit. Don't panic, you will live through the process and eventually feel less burdened by the siege mentality. If they, or you, do happen to toss something that you deemed important, know that it probably wasn't.

Keep only one box of memorabilia.

If you have a fear that you will eventually be left alone, that everything will be taken from you, then face that fear now and be the one to pass the items along. Be the one in control. Learn how to take control of a situation and let your self-confidence grow. That alone will release the clutter.

If all else fails, look at the nightly news and know that others around the world have lost their homes, goods, and families. Stuff is NOT that important, family is!

Clutter of the Mind

Once the clutter starts to accumulate, so the mind-chatter increases, and as it escalates so the ability to concentrate on projects and make good decisions, diminishes in direct proportion. And as the piles of clutter grow, so too does the inability to clear them, causing a vicious cycle.

Mind-chatter is probably one of the most difficult conditions to clear as it crosses from one emotion to another, then another, and another. It bounces all around according to what we are seeing, doing, or thinking. When connected to clutter, everything we look at screams a different emotion. Guilt. Anger. Blame. Unhappiness. Depression.

These clutterers get half way across a room and something grabs their attention, then something else, then another, and so it goes, and before long two hours has passed, but none of the clutter.

Nothing has been done. These were two hours that could have been spent doing something worthwhile, something tangible, something pleasurable. Now the mind-chatter escalates along with the guilt, along with the recriminations and head banging. "How could I have let it happen again!" Lost time. Wasted time.

They make coffee, read the paper, pick up a mindless magazine, make phone calls. Any distraction will do.

Connected to decision making, the emotional imbalance quickly turns into a debilitating state when the questions arrive: "Where should I put this?" "What do I do with that?" "Should I keep it or not?"

And as the questions clang and bang inside the head, the only alternative then seems to be to give up and do nothing.

If the piles, and decision making, have become just as overwhelming and paralyzing at work, however, then doing nothing is not an option, although, amazingly, many of these clutterers have clear heads at work but not in their own space, which means that the clutter is connected to home life—past or present

Mind-chatter is like a nagging toothache and we want something to deaden the pain. We want to stop banging our heads on that imaginary wall. But all that clutter reminds us that we are a failure. We can't clear the piles. We can't clear our own mess. We, in fact, are the mess! And as we survey the remaining clutter, we feel emotionally drained—and useless.

At which point we are too tired to do anything but sit in front of the TV or computer screen to take away the ache. We take a drink; pop a pill; make believe that our lives are as we want them to be, not as they really are.

The Remedy

Every time you pick up a newspaper, magazine, phone or piece of paper; ask yourself if it's going to further your goals. If it won't, don't hold it, read it or talk. If you don't have goals, now's the time to make some. Think about what you want your life to become. Start a project and keep it going to the end. Force yourself to do things that you don't want to do. If you are overwhelmed by papers, gather them from every surface and put them in one place, and one place only, then take a handful of them into a different area and work your way through them. Keep repeating the process. If clothes are the problem, pile them all onto the bed, then start to put them away. Do not give up until all the clothes are hung or folded back into drawers. If you find some that you really dislike, put them in a bag to donate.

Most people who listen to mind-chatter become so overwhelmed by life that they are unable to move in any direction, leaving the clutter to form a barricade. And mind-chatter is good at making you feel guilty, and the worse you feel the less likely you are to start the clearing process. You come in from the outside and it starts—tomorrow I'm really going to clear up, sort out, toss, donate. Tomorrow comes and the same ritual is

> ### SUGGESTION
>
> Join classes or organizations that will give you a different perspective on life. If you are overwhelmed with clutter, then find ways to connect to the outside world; otherwise the mind-clutter will build and stagnate. Let off steam by taking up a sport or a martial arts class, something active that will move you out of your head and into your body.

repeated. Again, again and again. Perhaps if I moved, you tell yourself. If I had a bigger space, more time, learned more in childhood.

But mind-chatter starts in childhood and usually comes from a judgmental parent or guardian. They give you praise one minute, then withdraw it with a negative the next, but it's the negative that you remember—always. Every time you look at anything, your mind swirls, connecting a negative emotion to it, one that has been left over from that childhood. Your life is filled with coulda, shoulda, wouldas. But you didn't—so cut the cord. Imagine having a string attached to the emotion that is disturbing you. In your mind, cut that emotion free and let it float into the air. Do this with any emotion that nags at you.

Keep practicing. Keep cutting. Remind yourself that everyone makes mistakes, even successful people, and it's not the end of the world—just look at celebrity magazines to see how many bad decisions can be made!

Make a decision about what you really want. Not a watered down version to suit someone else, but what YOU really want, and then stick with it. But keep cutting the emotional ties.

You are probably still surrounded with clutter, however, and it's not going to go away without some action. So if you need help to really start clearing, call a professional. When you pay someone to help you clear the mess you'll be surprised at how quickly the piles can diminish! Bite the bullet. Stop the mind-chatter. You'll also be surprised at how paying an organizer will kick start you into action after they've gone—and maybe even before they arrive.

You are not lazy, a slob, or unable to get organized, you are just too overwhelmed to make a start, and just as you'd hire a coach to help you get healthy and get your body in shape, so you can call a professional organizer to help you get your space in shape.

There is no shame in asking for help—especially when you are the one paying!

Control — No one to make you take action.

These clutterers, no matter what their age, believe that now they have their own space they can make a mess if they want to. They are not kids anymore and there's no one to tell them what to do. They can leave rotten food around, clothes piled high, papers everywhere, CD's and DVD's scattered around.

But making a mess is what children do, not adults, especially adults with self-respect. Their mothers may not be around to make them hang up their clothes, wash the dishes, put the CD's and videos back in the holders, or clean up their space; but finding things easily would be so much better.

This is more a control problem than a clutter one, and taking control of their area may be the only real power they have—or think they have. As a child, they may not have had a voice in any decision, but now in their own home they are king, or queen, of their kingdom, and they can be as messy as they like—especially if mother is coming to see them. This is often a way of getting back at some-one who constantly nagged them about being clean and organized, saying, "Don't make a mess on the floor" as the child was about to start an art project; "Money doesn't grow on trees" as clothes were piled on the floor, and "Take the garbage out" as they were going out on a date.

Even though many find wives, husbands or housekeepers to do their cleaning—or mothers who are willing to come over and wash the dishes, clothes and clean the home—this way of life doesn't create a rewarding, loving relationship or marriage. And in many cases it can provoke their spouses into a divorce.

And wearing crumpled and stained clothes can also put the brakes on a social life and career prospects, holding many back from promotions or from the career they really want.

And lack of control at work, or with coworkers, will often result in taking it where they can—at home—leading to a merry-go-round of looking unkempt and lack of career options.

Control represents resentment. Being against authority. Wanting to regain control over a situation that may in childhood have been out of control due to parents fighting, too many siblings with too many needs, or just trying to stay afloat in a chaotic household.

Some, with a control problem, grew up in homes where they had housekeepers to pick up and tidy their rooms, and never gave a second thought to how their homes remained clean and uncluttered. Now in their own space, being messy is just an extension of the control they already possessed in childhood—without ever realizing they possessed it. Control over a housekeeper who was paid to tidy up, no matter how big the mess.

And kids who had their creativity snipped in the bud as a parent berated them for making a mess, may have left their creativity behind, but the piles still remain. Piles of broken dreams that have now turned inwards and into an uncaring mess.

The Remedy

Maybe your parents had control at home, especially a mother who controlled the environment, telling you "not to make a mess," "to clear up after you," or that "money doesn't grow on trees," referring to not only to your clothes but everything else you left out, and you resented every word. But what you most resented was the control, control they had over you and control that you didn't have.

Now that same power has probably passed to a boss, coworkers, wife/husband, girlfriend/boyfriend, anyone you think has authority over you. And now you want to get back at anyone and everyone for that perceived lack. But your lack of control has caused the clutter to accumulate, and the very thing you resent others for, taking control over you and your life, is the very thing you are handing back to them by not clearing the clutter. Dealing with it could lead you to a much more productive—and probably profitable—life, giving you the control you seek.

On the other hand, if someone has become a doormat to you and your mess, then bitterness and resentment will grow on both sides, leading to arguments and anger.

If you have little authority at work, then decide to move up the ladder so that you have more control over your time and space.

You don't have to remain unkempt and resentful in order to feel you have free will.

Do you want something better, or to continue living in squalor? Do you want to feel victimized all your life, or feel your life is your own?

If you were given too much responsibility when young and you now don't want any, learn where the dividing line is between being over-whelmed and having self-respect. Learn that being messy is not about relin-quishing responsibility, but about being responsible to yourself.

Getting married, moving to a better job, being tired of constantly wearing crum-pled clothes, can all be a motivation to move on to better things. Turn it around. Start clearing the piles. Hang up the clothes, wash the dishes, take out the trash, put away the CD's, and see how good it feels to have con-trol of a space—your space.

> ## SUGGESTION
>
> Clearing the mess is about re-gaining control of your space, but more importantly, it's about having authority over the direc-tion you want your life to take. Make a list of all the things you have control over – and see that as a positive step – then write a second list of things you'd like to have more control over. Pick something small and achievable from that list, and take action on it. Work from the easiest and quickest, like a wardrobe or hairstyle change, to the harder ones, a change of job, home etc.

When you gain dominance over your living environment, you start to gain control over other things, and eventually that authority grows into a more positive outlook and less confrontational attitude, which will lead to better relationships—in both your personal and professional life. This in turn will lead to better career choices, better prospects, and better relationships with family and friends.

Being confrontational and defensive about your mess takes energy. It's like constantly having to guard your kingdom, which is why wars are fought, but it's energy that could be put to better use.

Isn't it worth it to change, and feel in charge?

Depression — Dropping away from the social scene

Which comes first, depression leading to clutter, or clutter leading to depression?

To a depressed person with clutter, the answer doesn't really matter. All they know is that both are affecting their emotional state and both need attention in order to move beyond it.

For most clutterer, however, it becomes a vicious cycle, since the more the clutter forms the more depression sets in, leading for many, to a paralysis in dealing with it—and leading, of course, to even more clutter.

Depression leads to apathy and lethargy, and beyond the immediate family, these clutterers are seen as depressed people who can't or won't pull themselves together. And even though the symptoms of depression are not limited to clutter, and certainly not that easy to deal with, depressed people often tend to push the wrong button in those who are not depressed and who have little real understanding of the symptoms—causing those who are most needed to walk away from the those most in need. This is especially evident in work situations where workers are expected to leave their private lives—and emotions—at home, and in families where children are taught not to express their emotional turmoil.

Most chronic clutterers suffer from some form of melancholy, even though it comes from different sources; the difference here, however, is that depressed clutterers usually become immobile. Most are unable to motivate themselves to do anything more than pop pills and eat junk food, to make them feel better.

They are the couch potatoes, computer addicts and magazine readers, who although they may profess not to need help, are knee deep in clutter, piles of Internet bought "stuff," and unopened mail. They buy every celebrity magazine available, seeing it as a way to live vicariously through the rich and famous and as a way of dealing with lives supposedly going nowhere.

Unfortunately, buying magazines and other things connected to an imaginary life also keeps the clutterer knee deep in mess, and often in debt, as more and more "stuff" bought on the Internet in the early morning hours, arrives weekly in order to alleviate the head-banging and the reality that their lives are not the lives of a celebrity.

As they retreat further and further into seclusion, the clutter is then seen as the reason not to become social, often disregarding the depressed state as the real cause.

Depression is usually a cry for help, but often when the help arrives, in this case to clear the mess, it is rebuffed, as small decisions turn into big decision and then the big decision turn into an inability to make any decision, so nothing is moved, cleared or donated.

Depression is stagnation, and stagnation of things, become piles of clutter.

The Remedy

If you are depressed and knee-deep in clutter, then open the door and admit you need help—then let it happen. Find a therapist or self-help group. Call an organizer. If you are feeling lethargic, force yourself to move. Go out and walk, exercise, anything that will jump start the energy. Once an action happens on one front it will automatically move you to take action in other areas of your life. Force yourself to be more social. If you don't like going out, invite people in—a great motivator to clear the clutter. See how your spirits are lifted and how much calmer you feel in the space when the piles diminish.

If you are a couch potato, or an Internet junkie, or a drinker, or a pill popper, you are probably not eating enough nutritious foods and have little desire in preparing fresh food. This is the beginning of a downward spiral of eating more packaged foods that have little nutritional value, which then leads back to more melancholy moods and little desire to do more than sit glued to a screen. So, instead of the usual chips and junk, eat something nutritious which will serve you better. Start to cook and take an interest in foods, and if you have the money, take yourself out—or meet friends—one evening a week to have dinner. And make it a ritual.

Clearing clutter is a great form of therapy and a good workout. It's also very cathartic. Do not see the entire space as one big cluttered mess. See it in small chunks. Room by room, area by area. Start at one point and work around the area. The door section is often the easiest starting point, so clear the surfaces from that area and then move inwards. Keep moving into the space in small chunks. Put all the papers together in one place, clothing together in another, all the bits and pieces that you don't know what to do with in another area. If you find things that you don't want to keep, place them together in a bag for donating. Put garbage in another bag, gifts to friends in another.

SUGGESTION

Sit down in a quiet place – without the TV, computer or music playing – with a recycling can and and shredder in front of you. Take 10 unopened pieces of mail. Open them one at a time. Is it junk, a bill, or something to save? Make a decision on each piece of paper and put it in the appropriate container: recycling, shredding, a bill to pay, or something to file. Repeat the process whenever you have a few minutes of free time. Action is the best antidote to depression.

If family and friends do come over to help, don't constantly tell them not to touch anything, but do be assertive if they try to toss something out that is very meaningful to you. Set boundaries; doing so will also make you feel more in control of the situation.

For well meaning family and friends: the best thing you can do for a depressed clutterer is to talk the person into having a professional organizer come into their home—even for a couple of hours. Start the process slowly. Usually the clutterer is so relieved to have someone there to help—especially a nonjudgmental person with no connection to their possessions or family—that they will allow the process to unfold.

Don't walk away and think they'll get over the dark mood. What depressed people really want is to have human contact and some form of help, without their having to ask for it.

These people are often not good at expressing their wants and needs, as most of them don't really know what they want—which is often the reason for their depression and piles of clutter. So, if you know someone who is depressed and surrounded by piles, be kind—and especially, be nonjudgmental!

Also read # 22--Shopaholism, and #23--The Overeater.

Being Creative - "Out of sight - Out of mind"

For years, people lumped together all clutter bugs, disregarding the fact that dealing with clutter depends largely on whether the clutterer is left- or right-brain oriented; making one size fits all organizing definitely inappropriate. Thankfully, this understanding is slowly starting to permeate through the clutter world, although there are still many who think that clearing clutter requires that "things" be hidden behind doors, under lids and in boxes.

To a creative mind, anything and everything grabs their attention and must be hoarded accordingly. And because everything is so important, all those objects, papers and oddments, should be saved, because at some later date, this, that or some other project—real or imaginary—will take place.

These are the people who are interested in everything and collect accordingly. They have so many projects and interests going on at once, that to see something not related to an ongoing project, will merely put it out of their minds as new ideas and projects are started.

Repeated reminders from family and friends to stick to one thing, are instantly dismissed, leaving their lives and rooms/homes/offices, a complete mess. Clothes are stacked and hung from anything that resembles a hook; papers are piled on every available space; sports equipment litters the floor, and creative projects are everywhere.

These individuals make every excuse for their accumulated mess as they cling to the image of a bohemian, an artist, a mad scientist, and to the idea that being creative necessitates that they live in cluttered spaces, no matter how debilitating the clutter may become. When creativity manifests, they will need "stuff" in order to live it!

These clutter bugs have homes piled high with newspapers, magazines, objects found on the street, furniture that was just too good to pass up, and other assorted things of interest.

They fill every square inch so that the kitchen cannot be used to cook food, the bedroom cannot be used to sleep in, the couch cannot be used to lounge on, the bathroom cannot be used to take a shower. And the pathway connecting all these spaces, narrowed to a walkway the width of a shoe - I kid you not!

Their homes are fire traps with no quick way of getting out if anything did happen, which is reason enough to clear the clutter, and the reason they often find themselves at odds with their landlords. These are people who need to see what they have, otherwise, projects just keep piling up with no end in sight and with nothing ever finished.

Think how many unfinished projects are found after the death of successful artists!

On the positive side, these artists give us dance, music, entertainment, the written word; and all the other wonderful things that bring joy to our lives. And they would give us much more if only they could find the things they need to start the project!

The Remedy

"Out of sight, out of mind" is certainly true for these creative people. But how much more could be accomplished if they cleared their work space and finished projects.

Fill your work and living space with plastic containers, containers with drawers, plastic boxes—small, medium and large—plastic zip lock bags, all sizes, for smaller things and cables. Closets that open wide are a necessity, although, in older homes, closet doors are usually narrow, with the inside space stretching out each side beyond the door and behind walls—making the space unusable for anything other than rarely used items.

If objects do have to be hidden for business or professional reasons, then make a cross-reference system so that everything can be remembered. Use lots of notice boards, big calendars, easy access filing systems, open boxes for equipment and other stuff. Use anything that will jog your memory towards the important things in life—like making a living and attending meetings.

But also ask yourself what's really important to keep and what you can let go. If you do need something for a project could you get it easily from another source? If you keep pictures and articles from magazines as reference, then set up an easily retrievable filing system. Use a hanging file—well labeled—for each category so that you have a place to put new papers and pictures as they come in. Inside the hanging file, place a plain folder; this is the only thing you remove when looking through the papers, leaving the hanging file in place. If you use this system you won't waste time constantly looking for where you last placed the hanging file.

Get to know where all your stuff is by having one place only for each item. It goes out of there, it's put back into that same place. If you are a "creative" person who has a resistance to filing cabinets—seeing them as antithetical to creativity—then get over it, and make your life easier in the process. It's okay to be practical and will do nothing to weaken the creative spirit.

The bottom line here, however, is that really creative people who have attained success, are in fact highly organized. I witnessed it many times, and so the idea of having to live amidst clutter in order to be creative is an

> ## SUGGESTION
>
> Decide on one place only for each set of things. Put all writing things together; have a filing cabinet for necessary papers, a big plastic box for staple guns, staples, packing tape, rubber bands, and anything else used for holding things together. Put all clips together in a smaller plastic box or tray, and use other individual boxes for all the similar things that you use for projects. AND – label them. What comes out, must be put back into its appropriate place.

excuse, and the sooner you let the image go, the closer you will come to being able to use your creativity to become a success—unless you fear success, in which case read #4.

Time spent looking for "stuff" takes away valuable time from being creative, so ask yourself what you really want your life to become, and then start the process to make it happen.

10

Too Overwhelmed to make a start

Most people with clutter are overwhelmed in varying degrees, but this is about being overwhelmed to the extreme, being paralyzed.

A large percentage of people who are at this point are often diagnosed as being depressed or having ADD—Attention Deficit Disorder—meaning that they can't concentrate long enough to start the clearing process; or anything else for that matter. These are people who have feelings of being emotionally swamped and not understanding why. But being overwhelmed leads to inaction, then a feeling of being a failure, which is often worsened by well-meaning family and friends who tell them to snap out of it and start clearing up.

But feeling overwhelmed is not the same as a debilitating depression. This is muddled thinking in the extreme. An inability to line up all the ducks in order to shoot them down one at a time, being unable to think in a linear way. It's also not the same as being creative and having too many projects going on at once. Creative people with too many projects are usually just too interested in all that life has to offer, whereas people who are deluged with conflicting emotions are just trying to hold on to life.

Also, for many people, being overwhelmed at home extends to being overwhelmed at work, with failure there adding to the pressure at home. Others can function at the office but not at home, which ultimately means that the emotional problems are connected to the home, and work is a release where they can relax and perform.

Dissatisfaction at home usually indicates that the problem is connected to someone there, or close by. A nagging husband or wife, mother or mother-in-law who make them feel inadequate. Family members who may all be tugging at their time and telling them what to do, while never acknowledging what they actually can, and do, do.

Usually, these clutterers were overwhelmed emotionally as children; often given too much responsibility at too young an age. A pattern set up by a parent or parents who had no way of dealing with their own burdens and passed along the responsibility to the child.

If the clutter problem is at work, however, it may be that the workload is too much or that coworkers are causing a rift in the office, leaving the clutterer to muddle through different emotions as they all clang and bang together and with no one to talk to to sort them out. No way of seeing exactly which problem, is the problem.

Then there is the guilt at not being able to clear the mess alone, the "I should be able to do this on my own" syndrome. Mind-chatter that keeps going around and around until it becomes debilitating, leading then to an inability to take action and more guilt.

The Remedy

Mind-chatter is set up at an early age and you've probably been living with it for so many years that by now it has become second nature. Seek professional help, either by hiring a coach/organizer or to join something like Clutterers Anonymous. Know that you are not the only one who feels overwhelmed, and even though many doctors have now latched onto clutter as an Obsessive-Compulsive Disorder, what you really need is someone to take you by the hand and give you guidance to begin the organizing. It's a hands on activity, which once finished, will make you feel more in control.

If you want to start clearing the clutter alone, then start small. Don't look at the entire mess as you'll become too overwhelmed. If papers are the problem, then take a small bag of them—along with a couple of plain manila folders—to a park, coffee shop, anywhere where there is no connection to you and your mess, then sit and go through them. Put the important papers to file or pay into one folder, and things that need shredding into the other, then bring everything home, including the papers to recycle. Repeat the process often.

SUGGESTION

Learn to have more fun in life. Take yourself to a movie occasionally. Give yourself permission to take a trip you've always wanted to take – and in the process learn how competent you really are. Don't take on more tasks than you can actually do comfortably – no matter who tries to make you feel guilty. And learn that really useful word, "NO!"

If clothes are the problem and you can't make a decision on what to keep and what to move out, call a friend. Try everything on and ask their opinion. If it doesn't make you feel great or look fabulous, ditch it—even if it was expensive.

If office clutter is the stumbling block, then go into work on a weekend, or after office hours, with a professional organizer. Surprise your coworkers on Monday morning and then see the clear area for what it is—a fresh start. From now on however, resolve not to take on a bigger workload than your fair share. Clear your desk at the end of each day and get instant gratification. Keep a well run filing system. If you start to feel overwhelmed, concentrate on what happened just before that feeling. Do you constantly feel anxious when papers mount up? When someone gives you a new project? When someone asks you if you have finished a project? Learn what, and where, the trigger points are. Practice clearing the mind-chatter whenever it appears. Learn meditation to calm your mine and read self-help books on anxiety and how to overcome it.

If you feel overwhelmed at home because of personal reasons, try and sort out why. Do your in-laws, parents, husband/wife, kids, friends, expect too much from you? Find the cause that produced feelings of being engulfed, a time when you probably felt that you didn't have the skills to deal with a problem: the death or illness of a parent or sibling, poverty, abuse, personal illness? Was it really your problem or a problem you took on because an adult couldn't, or didn't have the skills for it? If the latter, stop feeling guilty. Know that you were too young for the responsibility, and if failure did occur, you couldn't have stopped it.

Very often, kids who were burdened, have a difficult time making the right decisions later in life as they didn't have role models to teach them the skills. You are no longer that child, but an adult with your own needs, so start to enjoy the things that you missed.

Become more playful. Do fun things. Enjoy life more.

11

Not having a system

In order to set up a foolproof system
everything needs its own space, and
each time an item is taken out, it must
be put back into that same place. That's
a system. And all things need a system
just as we all need a home. Most people
have to be trained to follow a system,
however, which means that someone
has to implement one in order for others
to follow.

The cry "My family leave things everywhere" definitely
means that some sort of structure needs to be set up—by
the person who usually has to pick up the debris.

People who don't have a system are usually the biggest
complainers that their kids, husbands/wives and housekeepers creates a mess, when really no one has any idea
where items should go. And how can they know where to
put things if the household doesn't have a system to follow.
How many things become lost each time someone cleans
or does laundry? And how long does the family have to
spend tracking those lost items down?

Imagine hospitals without organization. Now imagine a

nurse beginning a new job there, and suddenly the others workers hear, "Oh, I'm sorry. I'm just hopeless at following a system." How long would they last on the job? How long would the patient live! And if drugs or instruments are missing in an emergency room because someone has misplaced them, then how many unnecessary deaths would occur?

Order has to be created, not by someone waving a magic wand, even though most clutterers wish that were so, but by someone in the household. And now that many families have two working parents with baby-sitters, housekeepers and other people coming and going, then having some sort of order in the home is essential. If one person doesn't know where another has placed things, then not only is time lost, but the household often dissolves into chaos, resulting in missed appointments, time wasted and frustration all around.

Most clutterers want some sort of system but are either unable to set one up or make excuses that they could never stick with it, which becomes a self-defeating attitude before anything moves. And lack of an individual system at work usually breaks down any kind of overall system for the rest of the office, leaving the same people to pick up the slack, leading to resentment.

A system should be put into practice from the top, but if that is not forthcoming, then one should be slowly implemented as a group effort. One that accommodates everyone.

Systems are not just for conformists and the running of a business, but for anyone who wants more time and an easier life—which hopefully, is what most clutterers want too.

Remedy

When you implement a system, then people at work and home will follow it—especially if it seems to be in their best interest. Systems are really about time management, about how much time you waste looking for lost items and how much frustration you want to endure.

Want to find out? Spend a week writing down all the time you squander looking for lost items at home and work.

To set up a system, start the process by asking yourself where you want things to go?

Do you have a place for laundry?

A cupboard for linens only?

A place just for toys?

Are the closets divided into separate areas for different types of clothes—T-shirts, pants, jeans......?

If you have deep cupboards in the kitchen, put appliances that are not often used to the back. Rotate foodstuffs as the supermarkets: new tin cans and packages in the back, old in the front.

If you hang garments, make sure that each item has its own hanger. If you double up then it becomes time lost, plus frustration and the beginning of a new pile as the other garment(s) on the hanger are left lying around.

And all clothing in drawers should be folded. It takes up less space; meaning you can get more into the drawer. Organize drawers according to types of clothing: sports clothes together, tank tops together, shorts, underwear, socks.

Put all things of the same type together, not in three different places so that you have to hunt for them—the reason many clutterers have three staplers and no staples, and four three hold punchers with only one actually punching out three holes in the paper.

Don't buy numerous boxes to store things in; if you stack them, you'll have to keep moving them around in order to get at the one you want—usually the bottom one.

Don't buy accordion folders for papers; they are a magnet for papers that will never see the light of day again. Instead, buy hanging folders and something to put them in, like a filing cabinet or a plastic hanging file box, and file your papers away.

If you live alone, then you don't have to consider anyone else using the system, so set one up that works for you. Don't listen to friends or family unless they have good ideas that agree with yours. And if you can't set up a system on your own, call an organizer to help you, and once it's set, keep it up.

Don't you have better and more enjoyable things to do than hunt for lost items?

12

"I don't have a shredder!"

If I had a dollar for every client who didn't have a shredder, I could have retired early!

You would think that in this day and age when identity theft is in the air constantly, everyone would have some type of shredder. But not so. I was constantly amazed at how many clients either didn't have one, or didn't use the one they had—and how many of them were well educated professionals! And some had already encountered problems with identity theft. So how to explain it? Denial? Laziness? Removed from reality? Naivety?

One of the first question I ask clients, when called in to organize, is "Do you have a shredder?" and probably six times out of ten they answer "NO." Or, they have one but never use it. Instead, they told me they tear papers up; meaning anyone going through the garbage could piece them together with ease. But what makes these successful, worldly people take such chances? And do they really have the time to tear papers into small pieces?

Not having a shredder denotes a total disregard for the reality of a situation, with no link between them personally and someone who wants to steal their identity. Is this why identity theft is so easy? These are often the same people who keep their passwords on a post-it note stuck onto their computer—and then wonder how someone managed to "break -in" to it.

I've found that there are three main reasons for this Pollyanna mentality. They believe in the "not me" syndrome. "It happens to other people."

Or, "I have nothing worth stealing."

Or they feel "I'm so rich they wouldn't dare!"

Pre-approved credit cards in the mail contain a lot of information, so to toss the entire thing, unread, gives that information away to anyone willing to sift through the basket/container/recycling bin and open a card in their name. Having to repair credit can take months, even years, ruining reputations and economic status, and making the purchase of a car, house, trip, or a medical emergency, into a disaster.

Many people also keep their personal papers at work, using the excuse that they spend more time at work than at home, which may be true, but with no locks on the drawers, are an open invitation to anyone who comes by. Passports, banking information, investment papers, medical records, personal letters, all are an enticement to peek. Do these people know who cleans the building after hours? Who the security guards are? Who wanders into the offices to work late at night?

Common assumptions are, that the cleaning staff doesn't speak English, doesn't understand technology, doesn't have time to go through the trash. But are we so frantic as a society that our own personal information is the last thing we think about? Or is it convenient to delude ourselves because of lack of time?

Remedy

Never, never leave any personal information at work, and never leave personal documents accessible, anywhere, any time. If time is the problem, then leave work a few minutes early some evenings and catch up on paperwork at home. Do the bills on a weekend. Get into a routine of taking an hour every Sunday—or some other allotted time—to do paperwork. Make it a habit, and include it into your time-frame for the week.

Having to repair personal information can take months, even years, requiring an enormous amount of time in phone calls, filling in forms, writing letters and e-mails, all diverting hours away from the things you need, and want, to do.

> **SUGGESTION**
>
> Why would anyone let others purchase an expensive item at their expense, while denying themselves the chance to purchase an expensive item themselves? That's basically what losing your identity does – it allows others the joy of buying, at your expense!

When shredders are so small and inexpensive, why wouldn't you have one? And if you do have one that you don't use, ask yourself why? Do you feel protected that nothing can get to your personal information because someone else is guarding it—doctors, hospitals, accountants, corporations, governments? Are you so rich that you think it couldn't happen to you? Are you so out of touch with the world that you don't think it could ever happen to you? Do you think identity theft is overrated and irrational? Do you think your computer is safe because you have all the latest security software installed on it?

If you believe any of these things, then know that you may be turned down for buying anything, small or large, if your credit has been wrecked by a thief—and you may not find out until you go to use your credit card, or open a loan to make a major purchase.

Get into the habit of opening the mail and sorting it immediately. Recycle the junk, shred the names and any other pertinent information. Keep the stuff you need and file it later. Try to stick to the old adage—handle it only once. AND take all personal information home—where it belongs.

No one wants to think ill of others, and equality is so ingrained in society, especially now with political correctness, that it leaves people vulnerable to the truth—that people from all walks of life, colors and creeds, lie, steal and don't give a damn about You!

Check your credit rating each year so that you know what's going on. Don't wait until you've decided to make a major purchase to check it. Credit scores are often wrong because the information in your file at the major credit rating business is wrong. But how will you know if you don't check it often enough?

Your character is your business. Their business is selling information—yours!

13

Big home. Big car. Big space.

To those with too little space, the thought of having too much seems laughable. But we do tend to expand according to the size of the area. And as people have become more affluent, so the size of their space has expanded with that wealth; into large homes, large offices, large entrances, and large cars.

But too much space, together with too little restraint, spells too much of everything, and too much of everything eventually grows into too many piles and too much clutter; in other words, too many unnecessary things.

How many CD's, DVD's, toys, strollers, clothes, appliances, cars, do we really need?

And just because there is space, why do we feel a need to fill it?

For many people, however, too much can be just as overwhelming as too little: too many things to buy, too much time spent moving from one space to another, too many people to employ to keep the space looking good, and too many hours spent working in order to keep all the "too many" going.

It's difficult to tell rich people they have too much stuff though, as many of them have worked hard to become this rich. They want things to show their friends how wealthy they are; otherwise, how else will they know? So every square inch must be filled, inside and out.

We have bigger and bigger homes for smaller and smaller families. Homes filled with "stuff" to compensate for being overworked. We fill the landscape to make sure that nature understand that we own it, rather than letting it support us. And we want bigger cars—with more and more stuff inside; TV's, DVD players, map readers, and bigger seats for bigger people.

Space, as many of us have been brought up to believe, equates with wealth and happiness. And the ads tell us so as they push the image that we should all move into bigger homes, with bigger mortgages, so that we can take out bigger loans to buy bigger stuff. And just as most people dislike silence and must fill it with words, so, too, space must be filled. These clutterers dislike having free time, a free room, a small home, or a small anything.

Space also represents boundaries and often these people had few rules to guide them when growing up. Now that they're adults they're not sure where the boundaries exist, leaving them uncertain about how to set them, either for themselves or their kids.

Often emotionally deprived as children, but not able to verbalize the void they felt, they now fill their lives with bigger and bigger things to compensate. And children from rich and poor backgrounds often respond the same way.

These people move stuff out of the house to the garage, then to sheds, then to bigger sheds, then to storage spaces, then to even bigger homes.

No space, for these collectors, is too big to fill!

Remedy

Life isn't a race to fill space, and just because you have it, doesn't mean you have to fill it.

If this is who you are then rethink your relationship, not only to space, but time too. And if you didn't grow up with boundaries, set your own by doing something that requires you to understand those perimeters.

Time represents space—as in the amount of time needed to manage a space—so learn how to organize both. Volunteer your time and set limits so that you have to be responsible for your own actions. Donate all the excess in your home to places that can reuse the items—but be the one to do it.

Space is like sound; it can be frightening or it can be

> ### SUGGESTION
>
> If you go into a gallery, museum, or a modern building with a hugh entrance, how do you feel – grand, opulent, important? Do you feel the same way in your large cluttered space? Or, do you feel small and insignificant? Does a large uncluttered space make you want to fill it with stuff, or, does it give you a feeling of freedom? If that's the feeling you want to keep, then unclutter your space.

Big home. Big car. Big space.

soothing. If you constantly have to have sound around you, with the TV on, music playing, talking to friends on the phone, then turn everything off and hear what life is like without the chatter. If open space represents insecurity, then start to allow yourself to experience life with less. Learn to live with fewer pieces of furniture, books and objects. Find out what bothers you about open space. Does it make you feel small? Insignificant? Afraid that you don't have enough?

Find the reason for wanting and needing more in your life. Not getting enough emotional support as a child, or felt you needed but didn't get it, may be the reason, and if it is, then find emotional support with others, either in a group or individually.

You're not that child any more. You're now an adult who can seek out what you need—unlike a child who is stuck with what they are given, or not given.

Maybe you grew up poor and are afraid of going back to that lack—of emotional support or space—and now that you have a big space of your own, you have this drive to fill it. As a kid you may have been given too much or too little, and now you're not sure how to balance anything. People respond to excess in different ways. Many kids who grew up with excess, still follow that pattern, while others take a different turn of not wanting any possessions at all, not even a home base.

Seek out your own balance. Read books that inspire you to downsize. Cut out photographs from magazines of homes you like and pin them on a board; use that as a springboard to having less. Take classes that lift the spirit—not the desire to shop.

Fill one small bag of clutter at a time to donate, recycle, or toss. Each bag will represent a small amount of unwanted emotional baggage that you've dragged along with you. Do it at your own speed. Move the boundaries closer to you until you know where they are, then work within them. You'll find that there is security in knowing where the perimeters are, and once found, will allow you to clear out all the excess and the unwanted. We give kids boundaries so that they can push beyond them—just a little—to enable their confidence can grow. Let your confidence grow with each decision too.

Change your friends if they are friends only because of your excess. Cut away anything and anyone who doesn't fit into your slimmed-down lifestyle.

Learn to love living with less—and love yourself more for doing it.

14

Lack of time

Often, what seems like a clutter problem is really a time management dilemma, one of where to put the time. These people don't grow piles from emotional issues—or so they think—they just don't have enough hours in the day. They are constantly on the go, traveling for pleasure or their job, working late, going to the gym, socializing, going anywhere, it seems, but home. They employ housekeepers, nannies, organizers, accountants, anyone who can fill in where they are lacking.

But lack of time grows from not understanding how to schedule the hours available and from an inability to know how to prioritize events in the first place. This is about time being taken over by important, or unimportant, issues—and knowing which is which.

Many of these clutterers avoid the clearing issue altogether by hiring others to do it, justifying the cost against their working, when what they are really paying for is someone

The EMOTIONAL IMPRINT of CLUTTER

to fill in for their lack of delegating skills and lack of ability to prioritize.

If the clutter is just as much a problem in the office, then time, and where to put it, needs to be addressed there too.

Time management, for some, however, is a form of control, and making others wait is a way to take control of a situation where they may have little control otherwise. Many in low-paying jobs—or those with little self-esteem—often play these games, usually unconsciously, seeing it as their only way to control a work situation where they have very little power. But if constant lateness continues then being fired usually ensues—adding to their already low-esteem status. Breaking appointments or underestimating the amount of time needed for a project, are all symptoms of this problem.

But being late is also about giving power to the other side, which in a job interview, undermines the one seeking the job—something many don't understand.

Time management is also connected to self-motivation, which can affect the type of jobs chosen. Those who work for others but are left alone to work on projects, need to be able to handle responsibility and time well, otherwise, a work overload results.

And many who work for themselves often find that they aren't suited to a home office for the same reasons—they need more human contact and more time structure in their lives.

These people do better in a controlled situation, where they are told where to be and when to be there, which many self-employed people find out too late!

Lack of structure can also turn into mind chatter, which makes many believe that it's a clutter problem instead of a time management one; and women, especially, fall into this trap when they decide to run a business from home to be with the kids. But if time isn't carefully structured, then chaos ensues and the business will likely fail.

Wandering aimlessly around the home, picking up a magazine, glancing at it, moving on to something else, then to something new, being in constant motion, is a time management problem which produces the clutter, not the other way around.

Remedy

The question to ask, is why there is never enough time? How many times do you really need to go to the gym each week, or is it a place to hang out? Ask yourself if the real issue is time management, or just being too tired, apathetic, or single. Would a relationship make you clear the clutter? Do you really need to hire all those people, or do you just need to teach the kids to clear up after themselves? Is the issue that you don't want a screaming match with the family every weekend to clear the mess, or that you really don't want to be home?

If the clutter is from having too little time, then perhaps you need to reevaluate your life. Are you happy with your job, home life, social scene? If not, set about changing it.

How do you want to spend your time? If you lose the time now, will you regret it later? Or, are you really sabotaging your job and social life, by constant lateness, feeling that you don't deserve anything better?

Get into the habit of clearing clothes, papers and bills, once a week. Make the time. Make it a routine.

If time management is really the problem, then learn to delegate. If you hire someone to pick up your kids after school, then let them make appointments for the doctor and dentist, especially if they will be the ones to take them there. If you find it too difficult to delegate then maybe you like the control—which also needs to be addressed.

If your work place is cluttered and creeps into the space and time of others, then look at how papers—or whatever—move from one place to another. Does your secretary know where to find things? Does she have to spend time looking for papers? Do others in your office spend time covering for you? If so, it's a waste of everyone's time, so start a system that works for all. Papers should flow through the door, move around the office, back to the door and out again. If something has to be filed, make sure you have a filing system that is easily understood by everyone using it.

> ### SUGGESTION
>
> The great thing about time is that it's an equal opportunist. We all get the same 24-hour days. It's the way we choose to use those 24 hours that makes the difference between those who achieve, and those who don't.
>
> If you get lost on the computer and lose track of time wandering from site to site, then buy a timer and limit yourself. Time used wisely can move you ahead in life; time used unwisely, moves others ahead.

The same goes for the home, start a system that everyone can follow, if the the family can't find items they will either not do the job or go out and buy the same item again because they couldn't find the original. Make everything accessible and have one place for each item; and teach the family that it goes right back into that same space. If you do this, the family will eventually have fewer fights and more free time. Involve the kids by helping them to set up a system for themselves.

If time is constantly getting away from you; the kids are late for school, sandwiches for a packed lunch are never ready on time, the beds are never made, too much time is spent looking for recipes and not enough time on making them, then acknowledge that there is a problem. Make the packed lunches the night before, or set the clock for half an hour earlier in the morning to get everything done.

But don't make the kids late for school because you can't get it together; otherwise you'll just be passing along your bad habits to them—which is grossly unfair!

15

Being a perfectionist

Perfection, for these clutterers, is have feelings that things are never good enough, clean enough, organized enough, and in the process become so debilitated with self doubt that they can't begin to clear the clutter.

For these individuals, mind-chatter is constant, as they continue to strive for that elusive feeling, and it usually starts at a young age, often after getting praise for something but always with a negative add-on. But the negative negates anything positive that was said before, leaving the negative to be remembered, while the positive falls away.

But being a perfectionist usually requires having someone, or something to blame for falling short. "I could have done it perfectly if so-and-so hadn't intervened." or "If I'd had more time—money—tools.......I could have cleared the clutter, room, home."

To a perfectionist it's all or nothing, which usually means that either all the clutter has to be gone within a few hours—which is unrealistic—or that they won't even begin. "There's no way I can get all this cleared today" is a familiar cry, then they don't start at all because they don't want to feel like a failure if they don't achieve their unrealistic goal.

The imaginary head-banging generally begins early on in life as they beat themselves up for not achieving idealistic results, rather than trying for obtainable ones, and as the chatter escalates that nothing they do is ever good enough, the negative response from others remains. And if they don't hear a negative response from others, then they say it to themselves until they are unable to finish anything they start.

Being a perfectionist is not only debilitating, but usually leads to wasted time as minute details are obsessing over, leaving the bigger and more important ones, to go undone. They can obsess for hours about finding just the right container for an object, and then decide to make a special shopping trip when one cannot be found; stopping the clutter clearing in the process.

These people have a difficult time seeing the big picture, seeing only the minutiae that make it up. They could be successful at many things due to their diligence, but usually sabotage themselves by not being quick enough to pull it all together as they pick at the insignificant details of everything they do. They work agonizingly slowly at the initial details of a project, losing the time needed at the end to really produce a well finished job. As they obsess over inconsequential aspects of whatever they are working on—whether home or work-related—they remain oblivious to the hours being wasted as the work piles up.

And each thing they start goes through the same debilitating cycle, moving them further and further away from their goals—and their real abilities.

Remedy

Understand that perfection is a moving target and as soon as you think you've reached it, it moves—and will keep moving, making it elusive. Once the idea of perfection is given up, then the clutter clearing can begin, slowly, corner by corner. That way each small piece of the clearing process can be achieved to the highest level.

Stop blaming others and start taking responsibility for the mess. It's your mess and it's okay that it's there. Millions of people have clutter and it doesn't make you a bad person, nor will you be liked less for having it. If your perfection comes from a distrust of others doing things to your high standard, then learn to delegate. Give others some responsibility—even if they are unable to come up to your level of perfection.

> ### SUGGESTION
>
> Make a list of everything you've accomplished in life. What have you written? If you're like most people, your list of accomplishments will come from school and work. But what about giving birth, volunteering, owning your own home, taking good care of your health, your aging parents and your children. Change your perception of accomplishment and then appreciate what is already perfect in your life.

Start concentrating on the positive response, rather than the negative. Remember how good you are, not how lacking you feel. Let negative comments go by, and keep the positive ones close to you instead.

If you can, go back to your childhood and see where the impossibly high standards started. What made you feel the need to be perfect? Were you compensating for a sibling who could never do anything right? A sibling or situation that was a bitter disappointment to your parent(s)? Did you feel the need to fill that void?

Or were the siblings good at everything, leaving you to struggle in their wake.

Did your parents push you beyond anything you could realistically do for your age, leaving their disappointment as an imprinted on you. Or, were they a disappointment to themselves, and you saw that and vowed to do better?

Life isn't perfect and doing your best at any given moment, is good enough. Tomorrow you may be able to do better, but doing your best today is okay.

Be positive to others and let them be positive in response.

Teach yourself to move away from each tiny mistake that you make and stop beating yourself up for it. The words you said and wish you hadn't, are gone too, and it's too late to take them back. You said the words, did the deed, so don't obsess. The people who heard and saw, have in all probability moved on, and if they haven't, then it's now their problem to deal with, not yours!

Stop rehashing things that you did years ago. Let the images of the event go, along with the embarrassment that you felt. The cruel words someone said to you, are all in the past. Cut the cord.

Every time you want to rehash a conversation, e-mail or project, take a deep breath and let the words drift into the atmosphere. Keep doing this until the mind-chatter stops. Take control of the chatter and stop it before it becomes a cacophony of sounds clanging and banging around your head. Tomorrow is coming and it can't bring better things if you are still hanging onto yesterday's words, actions and criticism.

16

Procrastinator

Most of us procrastinate at some point in our lives. We should do something but find a multitude of things to do instead, like reading the magazine we just picked up to move. Like making more coffee. Making that phone call, taking out the dog, going to the store. Anything it seems, to delay the inevitable job at hand.

Most people are procrastinators at heart, but it's the degree of procrastination that separates an ordinary problem from a chronic problem. Procrastinating can cover a multitude of strong emotions: fear of being a success, anger and wanting to get back at someone, not feeling worthy; and all the little subgroups—I should, but I don't want to; I'm going to the movies instead; I'll clear up tonight.

Procrastination is a feeling of being stuck and the clutter is self-sabotage, helped along in this case, by inertia. It is knowing something should be cleared to make room for other projects, things, possessions, but not being motivated enough to do it. Often husbands, wives, mothers-in-law, friends, coworkers and others who constantly nag to get the clutterer to clear up, instead prompts inaction as a response. And the more they nag, the more debilitated the clutterer feels.

Clutter can sometimes propel people into a divorce, and procrastination can be—subconsciously or otherwise—a push for that action. Then the question has to be asked, "Do they secretly want a divorce?" Is this the only way they know of separating themselves and walking away—a push to move on?

Not paying bills on time can also lead to the same dire circumstances for many, and the same questions arise: will being thrown out of their home, force them to take charge of their lives? Is that something they may secretly wish for, something to force an action that they may otherwise feel unable to take?

Very often procrastinators become time wasters because of an inability to fulfill some action to completion, giving themselves the label others have already given them—and many creative people fall into this category. But sometimes procrastinators are simply too overwhelmed to make a start and then they become immobilized, paralyzed, need help, but are not sure what type of help to ask for?

Often, they are the ones who don't think they have enough to offer in any way, and feel useless at life in general.

Procrastination also goes along with fear: of failure, lack of money, fear of doing the wrong thing, making a mess of whatever job they are working on, not feeling secure about their own abilities.

When dealing with someone who procrastinates, it is helpful to remember that it may not be because of laziness!

Remedy

Pick a goal you hope to achieve—not a de-cluttering one, but a goal in life to shoot for. Then work backwards determining the steps needed to make it happen, then work backwards to dealing with the clutter and see that as your first job in obtaining your goals.

SUGGESTION

Get a clock or timer and then give yourself 20 minutes to sort the clutter. If you have papers and other general items on a table top, then start there. Sort them into piles according to categories – DVD's, bills, papers, magazines, banking stuff, things that belong in the kitchen, bedroom, bathroom. After 20 minutes, stop clearing and take the things into their appropriate rooms. Leave them there. Repeat whenever you have a few minutes. Once all the items are in the right room or area, then set up a system to accommodate them.

If you want to go back to school in order to get a degree so that you can get a better job, then set out how you'd achieve that goal. Look around at your home and determine what space you would need to make it happen. Would you need more bookshelf space? More table space? A filing system for your school papers? Less clutter so that you'd be able to concentrate more on your work? Fewer papers and magazines laying around?

Read books on self-sabotage and try to find out why you are so negative about wanting to start anything. What words do you hear that stop you from starting projects? Where did you first hear the words? Who said them; parents, siblings, family members, teachers?

The words, and the association of words with non-action,

probably began many years ago. Who said words that put you down? That told you, you could never get things right? That you were never good enough? That your work wasn't good enough? That you didn't understand enough? That you will never get it right—projecting the negative words into the future?

Think back to projects or actions that you started, and what the response was to those projects by the people who saw them. Within that context you will find the beginning of your procrastination. Did you finish something that you considered praiseworthy, only to be deflated by a negative reaction? Sometimes parents and teachers don't understand how important a positive response can be, and sometimes they criticize children as if they were criticizing an adult.

But you are no longer that child. It's all water under the bridge and you should see it as that. See the water flowing along and taking all the negative words along with it, out to sea, where they will dissolve.

If family and friends constantly belittled you for actions not taken, projects not finished, things you said you'd do, but didn't, then pick something to do now and see it through.

How to know if inaction is procrastination or forgetfulness, or some other reason?

If you have the money and don't pay the bills on time, it could be a matter of control, so see what the real problem is. Look at what you procrastinate about and what you do finish.

Do you finish things at work, but not at home?

All procrastinators are good at finishing certain things—the key to why you put things off, lies in what is not finished.

Start a positive word project. Collect all the positive words that people say to you and put them together. Write them out on cards and when you start to procrastinate, get the words out and look at them. Then start to clear the clutter—or anything else you have to do—saying those words to yourself.

Yes, you can be a success—if you are willing to finish projects!

17

Crisis Maker

Crisis makers force issues by leaving everything until the final moment, at which time, everyone around has to respond to the crisis by bailing them out and doing the work that the crisis maker was supposed to have done in the first place. It's really a cry for help and often starts during childhood where not enough attention was given to them, forcing the child to do the only thing they knew how to do that worked—create a crisis.

These people wait and wait until the very last minute to pay bills, find documents or finish projects. They create havoc at home with their families and at work with their coworkers, always needing help at the final moment before the boom is lowered.

Crisis makers have piles—of papers, clothing and anything else they will need someday. And they know that somewhere in the pile is just the document they need and they assume that they know just where in the pile it is. But they don't. Usually the pile is too big and too out of control to find anything; just like their lives.

Involving others is not only their way of getting attention, but also a way of being able to take control when they couldn't as a child, a way of gaining attention from people around them when they were feeling unimportant. It's also about not understanding boundaries—in life and in spaces. They know where the office boundaries end, but why should they have to toe the line like everyone else, when the cubicle next to theirs has a little space where they could put a few things?

But this behavior also shows a lack of respect for others, forcing family and coworkers to help—not with goodwill—but because of an impending disaster, when what family and coworkers really want to do, is let the crisis maker swing.

A project needs to be finished by a certain date. Each person on the team manages to finish their part of the project by that due date; the crisis-maker of course, hasn't, now it becomes a crisis for the entire team.

Often, these people don't know how to ask for help before a crisis occurs as they don't want to be seen as failures—which they surely will be when the disaster rears its ugly head—and so they wait.

They live in fear of one day not being able to scrape by, while at the same time producing yet another crisis that will make what they fear the most come to pass; being fired.

Crisis makers want to save the day. "I know it's a pile, but I can find the document in minutes." They are like the people who start fires, then rush in to save someone from the burning building.

Once the crisis is over and the piles cleared, will life be as exciting as just squeaking through? Who will they be? Will they be important? Will anyone see them as having worth? These clutterers crave excitement in order to feel important, while not being exactly sure about what's really important and what's not.

Remedy

The trouble with creating a series of crises, is that you become like the little boy who cried "Wolf": eventually no one believes you, or cares. So learn how to ask for things before the crisis arises. Read books on being assertive. Learn how to speak the language that others speak with regard to asking for promotions and the things that you want. Listen to how others ask for help.

> **SUGGESTION**
>
> Usually a crisis arises from lack of time, so learn how to work backwards from what needs to be done and determine how long it will take you to do it. For every hour that you think it will take, add on an extra 30 minutes. By doing this, you should arrive at appointments on time, have projects finished on time, and catch flights, buses and trains – without a crisis!

Learn how to deal with life—before it becomes a disaster. Clear the mess and keep it clear. Show your boss, family, friends that you can make it on your own. Turn the tables, take jobs that require more responsibility, not less—ones that require forethought and planning. Become a team player and learn to anticipate disaster.

Think the best, not the worst.

Work on feeling important in life and less like an appendage. Work on self-esteem, on knowing that there is an important place for you if you're willing to make the effort to go there. Would a better job and more money help you feel less like making a crisis to compensate for what you perceive as your shortcomings?

Creating crises may make you high for the duration of the crisis, but what of the low that follows? Creating one crisis after another is like being a junkie, craving the next hit to get the adrenaline pumping. But there are other ways of getting the adrenaline pumped—exercise, creative projects, being involved with something new and exciting.

Find what you really love and do it. No last minute disasters.

Learn to think ahead and anticipate; learn time management skills, and learn not to take the time of others. Learn what respect is, for yourself and others.

Go back to your childhood and replay a situation when you made a crisis happen. Replay the response and ask yourself if you need that kind of attention again. Did a crisis in childhood bring your parents, friends and others rushing to your aid? Did the other kids think that causing a crisis was cool? Something to be envied, especially when you managed to scrape through the disaster without being expelled? Were you the joker in the class, the one who took all the risks that the others didn't have the courage to take?

Now that you're an adult, wouldn't you rather have

attention for the right reasons rather than having people rush to your aid and being seen as someone who can't get though life without a disaster happening. Without someone coming to your aid because you need money for the rent check; because you can't finish jobs on time; because you get involved with situations you shouldn't?

Start to understand why you constantly need a calamity, and the applause, for just squeaking through yet another one, then clear the clutter and your mind—and be seen in a positive light instead of a negative one.

18

Not taking responsibility

"I don't care! No one can make me!" A
child, even as an adult. A child who always
has someone to clear up after them, no
matter what the problem. This is a person
who doesn't take responsibility in life or
business, and who doesn't want to do
their fair share of anything, anywhere.
And while the clutter mounts at home and
at the office, they wait for help to arrive.

These clutterers believe themselves to be different from
the masses. Brought up by devoted parents who told them
they were very special, they now wait for someone else to
clear up any problem they may have set in motion, just as
their doting parents did—or others now do.

And if help doesn't arrive fast enough, then they play the
"lost child" game, reeling in people to play the role of
Mommy or Daddy to their irresponsible, inside child.

If married, they often drag their families with them into
the mess, forcing their children to become the adults they
have abstained from being. They don't pay bills, or, do anything on time and feel justified for their inaction, believing
that it's up to others to save them from imminent danger.

And they have a book full of well used excuses to draw from. "How dare the landlord evict us/me. It's just clutter, not a fire hazard" is a familiar cry, while others—usually family—are left to deal with the consequences.

Some start businesses, especially home based, in the belief that they will prosper where others have failed, but as their inattention and lack of responsibility to the daily running of the business wanes, so too does the business itself.

This problem affects all colors, creeds and social levels, They are the princes and princesses of the world, and in business these people often become the "stupid" grand-children who lose the family-built business.

They are different, however, from the crisis makers in that they're oblivious to the fact that their inattention is dangerous to health, body and soul—and to those they have dragged along with them.

They lose their jobs, get evicted and constantly point the finger at others for their downfall.

And it's difficult to get these people to grow up, even after a catastrophe. These clutterers don't care how much mess collects around them; they will wait until others are so worn down by their inaction, that eventually others will do whatever needs to be done—or they will leave the clutterer alone. And when wives, husbands or kids leave, these clutterers never believe themselves to be the cause.

This is also a control problem, although, truly controlling people have an agenda; people who don't take responsibility feel justified in dragging others along with them for the ride. And they will always have someone to blame for their problems and they will always walk away believing themselves to be in the right. Also read #7 --Control

Remedy

It's time to grow up, and time for others to help you grow up by giving you boundaries and ultimatums.

Time to put the tantrums away and face reality. If you were so special, your life would be better, more productive, more fulfilling and prosperous.

You're not as great as you seem to think and you need to know that. You've put everyone through hell and now it's time to pay your own way and take responsibility for your life, clutter, mistakes.

SUGGESTION

Sometimes not wanting to take responsibility for anything, is really fear of failure. Step up to the plate – in the office or at home – and be the one to volunteer your time to something. Be the mover and shaker for once, and see how good it feels.

If clutter was a criminal offense you'd be given community service—so volunteer somewhere and realize how lucky you are. Stick with it. Don't do it once and then leave, because the real problem here is that you lack boundaries and have never had to stick with anything before. But you have also never felt good about yourself either.

The "I don't care" attitude really hides an insecure child who has never actually achieved anything on their own; so why not start now? Start taking responsibility for small things, and then bigger things. Start by organizing the recycling into the right colored bags and then take them out of your home/apartment to the collection place.

Watch how much better your relationships become when you think a little more about others and a little less about yourself. See how moving your attention onto the other person gives you more back in the form of their attention. Talking and listening should be like a tennis match, a back and forth between people.

Watch how many more things work out in your life, when you change, and watch how your self-esteem grows.

Start to clear the clutter, even if you have to hire an organizer to get you started—but don't rely on them to do all the work. It takes work to become someone special—and for others to acknowledge that you are special. So start to grow into the person you want to become. And age has little to do with this, so there are no excuses for being either too young or too old. Learn what real responsibility tastes like; give it a name, a name of something you like to eat, and whenever you see yourself backing away from responsibility, think of that taste of success.

On the other hand, if you dislike responsibility because growing up no one thought you were capable of it, then work on taking small amounts. If you were given too much responsibility and now don't want any, work through the reasons for your response.

Were you given too much as a child, and now resent having any? Even though your parents were doting, did you feel abandoned because they both worked? Did you resent that? Do you resent responsible people because they are responsible?

Take on more authority at work and surprise your coworkers. Start to see yourself as a team player - not a cheerleader.

19

Guilt - of having too much.

Remember as a child being told how kids in other countries were starving, and like most other kids, you volunteered to pack up all the foods you disliked to send to them?

Then we all found out that life doesn't happen like that. These do-gooders, very often, are still trying to be that kid who wants to send food, clothing, anything they think the world needs, to others. But are they really doing good?

These people are connected to #20 - The Family member who takes it all—but are different in that they take and store anything they think will be of future use, for friends, for people they barely know, for organizations. They take furniture, books, clothes and general clutter, and store it anywhere they can.

They are the dumping ground for friends, kids, parents, brothers, sisters, nephews and nieces, who all know where to take anything they don't want or need. Out goes the clutter from their homes, in comes clutter for the do-gooder. And they take the stuff even if they don't have room, are having a crisis, having a baby, moving, or just feeling overloaded. They feel sorry for others, no matter what the reason.

They feel guilty for having as much as they do in their lives, and that many in the world go hungry, have few possessions, lack education, or good health care. The list goes on and on. But they never question if those in other countries really want all the stuff we, in the West, have accumulated. If we are trying to downsize our piles, why would they want to increase theirs—unless it could actually do some good?

Guilt exudes from every pore of these well-meaning souls, extending to their kids, coworkers and anyone they feel is not doing their part. They sermonize, press the guilt button and play the "do-gooder" role to perfection. They tell their own kids to "eat everything on their plates, since in other parts of the world kids go to bed hungry." They want everyone in the world to have more. But do they ever question their own motives? Do they really act because they want to share and give, or because of their own internal emotional needs?

These clutterers desperately want to help, but are misguided about what the needs of others are and don't have a clear understanding of what they are going to do with all the collected "stuff."

They haven't bothered to do the research on what each charity needs and accepts. They know only that they must do something to help the less fortunate—and in their case, it's collecting "stuff" that others don't want.

Remedy

Cut the cord on the guilt and get the collected stuff out of your place and into other places that can use it. Donate, send, or put it on the street, but do it quickly. Donate to any organization that will take it—your good deed and your guilt free decision. Free up your home for your family, or, if single, yourself. It's your space: reclaim it and live as you'd like to live.

SUGGESTION

It's tough to watch the evening news and see all the misery in the world, but there are also hard-luck stories closer to home – closer to your home – so get involved there. Find out what people really need, and then find a way of getting it to them. If older people are afraid to leave their apartments, then take a couple of them together on food shopping trips. Take snacks and drinks and invite them to sit in a park and talk. Many people in need never ask for help.

And if you have excess furniture, then see who needs what in your neighborhood, and then get it to them.

Feel how good it is to live in a clutter-free home—and how clear your mind feels. Don't get sucked into feeling guilty about your having so much and others so little. Life is unfair, so find other ways to contribute. BUT, if you really do care about those less fortunate, then volunteer your time, or find ways to raise money to help good causes. That way the organizations can buy what is really necessary for those in need—like tents, blankets, clean water and food.

If you are keeping "guilt gifts" from aunt So-and-so, but you don't really like the item, your only obligation is to thank the person for the gift and then pass it along to someone who would like it or needs it. Get it out of your home to make space for something you would like better. If you think the giver will visit you one day and ask where their gift is, have an excuse ready for the item not being there, but don't get caught into their guilt trip as you say it.

Don't hang onto stuff thinking that one day you'll find an organization that will take your special item. You may wait a long time. Instead, move it close to the computer and list it on eBay or some other site—if you think it has value—but start the process of getting it out of your home. If guilt is the problem, then see the selling as a way to make money that you can then donate to charity. Put the unsaleable stuff by the door, ready to leave. And, when your family, church or friend asks you to take something, say the word NO. If it's too difficult to say, practice.

Give thrift stores—usually connected to some charitable organization—a chance to make money on your items while you get a tax break. Move furniture along to organizations that connect the homeless with homes of their own—and who will need furniture when they move in.

And ask yourself if you really feel guilt because of the plight of others, or because your emotional needs are not being met? What are you lacking in your life? Is all the collecting taking away from you having a loving relationship, and spending time with those people? Or, are you in a relationship that isn't loving, and doing good deeds fills that void?

What are your real motivations for collecting? What are you trying to overcome? Do you need to feel needed? Need to be acknowledged? Need a pat on the back? Were you the child who took on all the family guilt—while they had all the fun? If so, then it's time to cut the cord and find better ways to give back—teach adults in your area to read, tutor a child, help sort stuff at a charity store—instead of collecting it at your place.

And if you really do want to help Third World countries, then join The Peace Corps!

20

The family member who takes it all!

In every household there is always one person who gets burdened with all the family memorabilia, and it's usually the one with the least amount of space, often unmarried, usually female. These are the people who take it all because they know no one else in the family will, and they don't want to see the pictures, letters, documents and other assorted things disappear. And the family knows that they don't want to lose family related pictures, letters and documents.

Often, this family member moved into the position of caretaker during childhood, usually as the one responsible sibling who could be relied upon. Not necessarily the eldest of the children, but treated as a child older then their years by parents and other family members, giving them responsibility they were too young for, but took on anyway. The end result is that these clutterers now feel obligated to take the family memorabilia, even though they may not have families of their own to pass them along to.

They are a little like #19 - those who feel guilty, but this time it's about the destination of the family documents, and is usually more about obligation than guilt. There is always one sibling in the family who can be counted on to preserve what previous generations have saved, and often it's the child who wasn't destructive with their own toys, but had to share with the others, who were.

We are a society of hoarders and a large part of that comes from having parents and grandparents who lived through the Depression and remembered the sense of lack in their lives and the lives of others. And even if they didn't live through it, they taught the next generation not to throw anything away that might have a future use. Hence, the odd assortment of bits of string, bottle tops, corks, nails, screws and other "necessary" objects everyone collects in a drawer.

What that left us with, is an inability to throw anything away, even if we have the money to buy another, or can access more. And the mind-chatter rears its ugly head whenever we are close to throwing or donating something somewhere, or to someone.

And when it comes to family documents and photographs, the desire to dump the blurred photographs and unreadable pieces of paper, is usually overridden by a small voice that tells us that something bad will happen to us if we don't save them all—maybe in the form of a visitation of past family members tut-tutting their displeasure!

Remedy

The first thing to do, if possible, is to have a family meeting to discuss what's really important in the papers, photographs and documents. If the family can't get together, then have a conference call or e-mail everyone the same message.

Next, discuss where the memorabilia should be kept. If the conversation keeps returning to you being the guardian of the papers, stand your ground and explain that you lack the space, don't have kids, or don't have the time to take care of all the documents.

If the problem is more than documents, such as furniture and small objects, then make a decision on what's worth keeping and what isn't.

If there is someone else in the family with a larger place to store things, but who constantly makes excuses about why they can't take the stuff, and if the family designates them as the taker, then box the things and take them over, or send, or ship them.

> ### SUGGESTION
>
> If storing the family memorabilia has become a sore point in the family, then rent a small storage space for all the items, boxes, books, etc., and split the cost among the family members. The kids and grandkids shouldn't be denied a chance to see their past, because no adult wants to do their part in preserving it.

If they have refused in the past when the subject was broached, wait until a large family gathering occurs, and then take over some of the things, even if you have to fly the boxes to their destination with you in tow.

Present yourself, and the boxes, to the family and say that you just don't have room for them any longer. If there are younger family members, get them interested in the documents and photographs so that they'll see value in saving them.

If you've moved a number of times with the family things, often to smaller places, while watching your siblings buy bigger and bigger homes, then know that you have done your part to keep the memorabilia together. If the family does make a big deal about taking it, making you feel guilty on the way, know that you've been more than generous with both your time and living quarters.

Go through all the family things and keep only what will be truly important for future generations: birth, marriage and death certificates, photos of family members only— by the second generation no one remembers non-family members—important documents and letters. Then ditch the rest. If a large amount of things need to be kept, then rent a small storage space somewhere and split the monthly bill among family members. Very often seeing value in old things skips a generation, so usually the interest goes from grandparent to grandchild. See it as your contribution to their genealogy.

And as we watch natural disasters and wars occurring around the world on the nightly news, we all need to recognize that our stuff is not that important. Having a roof over our heads, food on the table and the love of family and friends, is really all that counts—the rest is gravy!

Too much information

We live in an information age where computers and technology were supposed to make our lives easier and less cluttered; unfortunately, just the opposite seems to be true.

This group of clutterers have information overload as they gather it from from far and wide: magazines, newspapers, free pamphlets, junk mail, articles printed from the Internet and information collected from the office and from shopping trips—all collectible information, and all important to the collector. And they are unwilling to give up any of it!

They fear not keeping up with every bit of information that's out there, and think everything too important to discard, and knowledge they should use or store. Very often these people not only clutter their own lives, but they also send magazine and newspaper clippings to family and friends, cluttering up their lives, too. The implication then is "I don't want to have to save it, and I don't want to throw it out, so I'm sending it to you to keep!"

They seem to think that if they don't keep every piece of paper that passes through their hands, they will miss something, something important, something others are talking about, something that will keep them out of the loop. And being in the loop is the very reason they save all printed matter.

They have mountains of newspapers and magazines waiting to be read. When, they don't know, but read sometime in the future when they have time. And as more information keeps arriving, the more the piles grow; to the detriment of health and safety, as many have learned too late when fires start and accidents are caused. And many, not content with filling their homes, will then fill up the garage, sheds, storage spaces and any other area that is available to them.

These are the news junkies needing to know, from every TV and radio station, blog and web site, what's going on around the world. They fear not having the information, not being able to contribute to conversations with others, being seen as less knowledgeable than most. But often, the more information they collect, the less time they have to really absorb the significant news; and more importantly, have little time to make their own judgments about what they are reading. They know what TV personalities have told them to know, what newspaper journalists have told them, what bloggers think they should know. But what do they really know?

And now with computers they can print things from web sites; pages and pages of more printed matter. More piles, more clutter. They are being crushed by information overload as it stops interaction with others, stops real debating about real issues and real listening to opinions of family and friends. Their lives are lived, and opinions formed, by others, leaving little time in their saturated minds to form their own opinions.

Remedy

It's difficult to tell a news junkie that tomorrow will bring more news, magazines articles, words on the Internet. But it will, so what if you don't have a fix for a day or two everyday? If you miss the newspaper one day, weekend, or week, what will you really miss?

Giving up information is like recovering from other addictions, it requires a weaning off process, a slow withdrawal from news over-load, which if not done can stop forward movement—quite literally—by a home filled with paper. And for those who don't share the

> **SUGGESTION**
>
> Join a library and go there to read magazines. Borrow books from there, too, so that you have a deadline to take them back. And practice leaving the magazines and newspapers of others where they are.

same addiction to news and information it can be unimaginable to have this kind of obsession, so think about how others see you.

If you really want others to think you are well informed, toss the paper load and join a group were you can discuss news items or other interesting topics. Drop the inferiority complex and the craving for respect—which drives you to collect—and spend less time reading, watching and listening, and more time on your career, which in the end, will move you up to a better position in life than all the Internet time ever could. If you want to make a name for yourself, start now with something you're good at. People will respect you more by seeing you do more.

Information is swirling all around and isn't going to disappear any time soon, so set up a good filing system—in an actual filing cabinet—and keep only a small number of articles. Limit them to the size of the filing cabinet and once it's filled, go back and toss. DO NOT buy more filing cabinets!

You will probably never travel to all the countries whose pictures you've cut out of magazines and newspapers, and if you do, chances are that things will have changed by the time you leave: the currency rate, hotel and air fares. Toss the item and get up-to-date information on the Internet when you do actually go to that foreign place. Same for health, technology, recipes, and anything else that you deem so important. Let it go, recycle all the paper; have faith that more will arrive tomorrow.

If you can't finish reading the entire weekend newspaper in a week, cancel your subscription. If you have magazines piling up waiting to be read, cancel them. Think of space in terms of money. How much space are your piles of paper taking up? If you know the square footage, divide it up into floor space and then divide your rent/mortgage by that number; calculate the real cost—not to mention how much emotional toll they are taking.

Can't toss all those unread magazines? Tear out the articles you want to read and staple them together. Then put them all by the door. Each time you go to the doctor or dentist or use public transportation, take one—and only one—article. Read it during the day, and then decide what you want to do with it: toss, file, or shred—gone!

Shopaholism

We usually think of clutter as being "old" stuff: piles of papers, clothes, appliances. But clutter also comes in "new." Piles and piles of new! And most of us know someone who's a shopaholic; friends who constantly spend and have closets full of clothes with the tags still on, make-up still in the boxes, unread books piled high. They also have bathrooms filled with lotions, pharmaceutical drugs, soaps and anything that they think will enhance their looks or their decor.

Shopping cuts across both genders, although men and women usually shop for different things. Men tend to buy antiques, technology, electrical gadgets, shirts, jackets and magazines. Women buy clothes, shoes, make up and lotions, and things for the home—cushions, sheets and other objects.

As much fun as it all sounds shopping can be a serious problem, as serious as gambling and other addictions—and just as destructive if it keeps a person in perpetual poverty, as it does for many. Most shopaholics don't have the means to shop until they drop, which doesn't stop them as they max out every credit card as new ones keep arriving. It's the feeling of being a kid in a candy store that keeps them buying. A kid without responsibility.

And that's the point for many of these people. When they go out they are dressed to kill, dressed for fun—while being embarrassed to invite people back into their clutter filled homes.

They rationalize their spending as buying a "bargain," or something "I need" or "will need in the future." "Buy now, pay later" being their mantra. They buy online, from the Home Channel, from junk mail promotions, from e-mail ads and from stores. It doesn't matter where they buy from, just as long as the stuff keeps coming! Closets are overflowing, new toiletries remain in bags, and boxes of unworn clothes and shoes are piled high. They have bags of stuff never unpacked, sometimes buying the same thing twice because they didn't remember that they'd already bought one.

These clutterers live in the future of what will be, not what is. They shop for the then, not the now. They shop to compensate for who or what their lives have become, feeling they haven't fulfilled their potential, no matter how successful or attractive they are.

While women buy things to make them more attractive, men buy to fill their homes with more expensive electronics and technological toys. It is a need to constantly upgrade, look better, have better, be better. They buy to compensate for what they think they didn't get as a child: time, affection, applause. They keep trying to build a nest by filling the external space, when really they are trying to fill the void within themselves.

This is a serious problem that affects their way of living, and if they are in a relationship or have a family of their own, can have serious consequences. And it doesn't matter whether they have money or are on welfare, they think spending will end their poverty, a bad marriage, fear of being left alone, or any other problem they have.

Remedy

A good way to know if you are a shopaholic is to look at how many tags are hanging from your clothes. How many appliances have never been used? How many lotions and potions have never been opened? How many shoes are still in boxes, unworn?

To know how serious your shopping habits are, count how many shirts, suits, blouses, pants, dresses, shoes, you have in your closet. Write down the numbers. Shocked?

If there is an overwhelming number of one type of clothing, pull them out and put them on the bed. How high does the pile go? How many items are of the same color? Same style? Most shopaholics don't know what they have in their closets, so they buy two or three of the same thing. What do you have in duplicate?

Do the same thing with all the types of items. Put all the lotions and potions together and then vow that you will not buy more until every last bottle has been used up: shampoos, face creams, make-up, nail polish. If you have half-used shampoo bottles, pour the contents into one.

Consolidate. If you have a number of half-used bottles of nail polish, mix them together. Make your own colors. Put blobs of the new color onto a piece of paper along with the name that's already on the bottle; that way you'll know what color is in which bottle. Have fun. There's nothing to say you can't combine colors, so be creative.

Put all the same type of drugs together in a small zip lock bag. Anything that has an expiration date that's passed, toss.

Ask yourself what you are compensating for? Love? Grief? Attention? Boredom?

> **SUGGESTION**
>
> If you have a large suitcase, take it out of the closet and open it up in the bedroom. Fill it with all the things you'd use in a week – clothes, shoes, bags, lotions and potions, books, magazines, and other assorted things. Now use only what you have in that suitcase in the following week. Don't cheat!
>
> At the end of the week take stock of how well you did – and how few things you actually needed for that week. Now see your shopping through different eyes!

Where did that come from, and why is it keeping you poor and/or cluttered? Do you like being poor? Did someone use money as a way of having power over you, parents perhaps, or a spouse? Do you see money as something that has to be "got rid of" as soon as possible because of the negative connotations? And even if you have enough money, why are you constantly buying? Was shopping passed down to you as a way to alleviate feelings of depression? What do you feel is missing in your life?

If you do have many items of clothing that are the same,

pack a few of them into boxes to use at a later date, when the ones you're now wearing start to look shabby. Now promise yourself that you will stop shopping, and that from now on you will only buy what looks good, feels good, does you good, and is what you really need.

The market is geared to obsolescence, but you don't have to be part of it, and neither does the planet. Accept that you are attractive enough, slim enough, tall enough, good enough. Feed the soul, not the corporations. And cut up—or cancel—credit cards! If you are tempted to buy something, take a day to think about the purchase, usually after 24 hours it won't seem so imperative to buy the item.

And, if you hate your job? Put plans into action to get a better one. Look at going back to school—even if you have kids. Others have done it before you; you can do it too

Also read #3—Not feeling worthy.

23

The Overeater

Overeating is a form of cluttering, a physical form that grows from the emotions much like other cluttering, and it too fills a need. The only difference is that it fills the body not the external space, and as the body expands, so too do the number of different size clothes, the ones they will be wearing again if only they can get down to that imaginary size 2 again.

Overeaters buy food the way others buy clothes, it's just that most of the food can be classified as junk. Real food is hard to find in their kitchens, while packaged foods, soft drinks and anything sweet, or high calorie, is plentiful.

They squirrel snacks away at work, just in case they should feel hungry during the day. And at home, they make sure that the kitchen cupboards and refrigerator are always filled with their favorite—mostly empty-calorie—foods. They buy the biggest bottle of soft drink because it's cheaper than the smaller size, large sizes of all foods so that they will never run out. They buy in bulk, then have to eat in bulk.

This mentality also plays a part in other forms of clutter

too, especially with regard to relationships and allowing others into their space. Overeating is a way of not allowing people to get too close as the body grows outwards, forcing others to keep their distance, at home and at work. Often taunted as a children for being overweight, these people turn the hurt inwards, making their bodies a void to be filled—in this case, with food.

But putting weight on also leaves many with a false sense of their size—the opposite of Anorexics—seeing themselves as slimmer than they really are, which then allows them to gorge even more. And just as they don't understand how much food they consume, so, too, they have little understanding of the space around them or how much volume their bodies take up, underestimating their width in relationship to chairs and other furniture.

Living in denial of how much they eat, leads to little understanding of the boundaries of their stomach size: how much food it really needs, or can comfortably hold. And being overweight is all about boundaries—all boundaries— how far the body can move, without getting tired; how far they can travel comfortably, in 'plane, train, bus and car seats; how far up the professional ladder they can climb.

As their energy declines, due to their weight, the piles grow accordingly, and the more the clutter grows the more they dislike their surroundings, which then leads them to buy magazines by the armful and to consume vast quantities of junk food as they read them; comparing themselves to the celebrities on every page, the ones who are young, slim and gorgeous—and hating themselves for eating their way to outsize.

Also read #5 - Fear not having enough.

Remedy

As most of us eat by the clock not by hunger, it's difficult to stop the habit of eating when others eat, especially when we have little control over our work hours and lunch times. But we can control what we eat at those times, so just before lunch, stop and close your eyes for a couple of minutes before you go out to buy food. What do you really want to eat? A sandwich, soup, a shake? Or would you rather take a walk and have a health bar?

> ### SUGGESTION
>
> A large bag of chips weighs about 5 1/2 ounces. Each ounce of chips equals 150 calories, so the entire bag contains 825 calories. Four bags equals 3300 calories. It takes 3500 calories to make one pound of body weight. If you cut out just one bag of chips per week, in four weeks you'll loose close to a pound of fat – 12 pounds of fat a year!
> Want to loose weight quicker, double the quantity.

Not in the habit of eating a health bar, then choose something that is healthy and satisfying. Nuts, cereal, sushi, a healthy snack?

Throw out the habit of eating certain things at certain hours. People in other parts of the world eat different things for their meals than what we eat in the West, so mix it up, have pizza for breakfast if that's what you want. Have a shake for lunch. If you feel satiated after each meal you'll have less reason to snack on unhealthy foods between meals, which is usually where the weight creeps on.

Keep healthful snacks in your desk if you think you'll need something later in the day.

Many overweight people make the excuse that they can't lose weight as it's their metabolism that's causing the problem, but very rarely is this true. What is true is that most of us in the West have bodies clogged with junk foods, which often cause more cravings for junk and sweet foods, which then overloaded the system, making us feel so lousy about our weight that we then eat even more. So start to eat fruits and salads in larger quantities and help unburden the system, feeling lighter and more energetic throughout the day. And if you always order an additional appetizer or side order, when eating out, cut it out. That alone will bring down your weight.

If you can't change your diet alone, get others to join you. Take a trip to a good health store and ask for advice about products. Take every free magazine and pamphlet on health that you can find. Read them, cut out any relevant articles, and recycle the rest. Start to understand about your own body and your own health. Make it a group effort. The better you feel, the better food you'll gravitate to. And if you have the money, go to a nutritionist instead of a gym; it'll do you more good in the long run. Be realistic about your size too. If you will never shrink back to the size you once were, ditch those clothes.

Start to clear the clutter at home and get your place looking the way you would like your body to look—sleek, well toned and attractive. Pick a pile that you can work on easily, then as the clutter dwindles notice how the desire to get in shape increases.

Tell yourself that you will become more social, and that you won't hide and camouflage your body under outsize clothes. Buy a garment that is totally against who you think you are—and wear it with pride. Watch the reaction of family and friends. Is it really you? Be brave, step out of the mold, take classes, read cook books—and stop watching celebrity shows on TV. Stop reading about celebrities and comparing yourself to them. Read about positive role models and then get to work.

And remember: there is no such thing as a perfect body. Most of them are airbrushed!

24

Not caring about others

Very little can be said about these people
except that they are selfish, and usually
labeled so. They are not team players and
have a difficult time relating to humanity,
even though they think they are. These
are people who genuinely don't seem to
care about others and who lack empathy.

Many were brought up by doting mothers who did everything for their Prince or Princess and expected nothing in
return. And it's the not expecting anything in return that
usually makes these people selfish. No demands. No pay
back. No responsibility.

And if they are married to someone like themselves, the
marriage usually ends in divorce.

They just don't understand what all the fuss is about and
why others think they are self-centered. They live in a fan-
tasy world, concocted by their parents, which has success-
fully kept them away from the reality of life. They don't
have the tools to understand what it means to be a team
player or how to involve themselves with others, leaving them with an underlying emotion of mistrust. Often,
hurt as children because of their lack of social skills, and

determined not to let it happen again, they start to built a wall around themselves.

Many are conflicted emotionally, with an underlying fear, usually stemming from an insecure childhood when they were never given the chance to learn how to deal with life on their own, and now needing to learn those lessons, are fearful of the responsibility that comes with the learning.

The insecurity can come from lack of money, having a family who constantly moved, lack of stability in the parental relationship—as in divorced parents—or being brought up in a chaotic home; but all with a parent shielding them from the realities of the situation. Many have been labeled Attention Deficit Disorder, which often stems from fear, nervousness, lack of awareness and an inability to find balance in their lives.

Inside every selfish person, however, is a smaller one trying to protect the outer one from everything and everyone, and having absolutely no trust in humanity and feeling the need to protect themselves at all cost, they become selfish and self-centered. And any attempt to help them—as in helping to clear their mess—is seen as a judgment against them and their abilities, even though they are good at making it appear as though they don't really care.

Underneath, these clutterers are insecure about their own abilities and really resent the parent(s) who have either coddled them for all the wrong reasons or have given them too few tools to work with in their adult lives.

Remedy

The only way back from being totally selfish is to listen to how others perceive you, and then start to uncover the reason why you act this way and why you have developed such a hard shell that nothing and no one can crack it.

Do you have a parent—usually the mother—who won't let you go? Does she hang on to you out of her own fear of being left alone? If the household you grew up in was chaotic, were you her only anchor? Has she passed that fear along to you so that you can't respond positively to others, leaving you now to see any request as controlling and every issue a confrontation. What would happen if you opened yourself up just a little? Would you be wounded by others? Is that what you fear?

If you are in a relationship, try to trust more by listening to the other person more. Don't take every little word personally. Learn how to listen to what people are really telling you and don't always see it as a negative comment on you or your life. Perhaps they're offering constructive criticism that will aid you in the long run.

> **SUGGESTION**
>
> Play a listening game – preferably with a partner that you know well – and see how many minutes you can listen to them before interrupting with something you have to say. Doctors take about 23 seconds before interrupting a patient. How long before you interrupt?

If the issue is from Attention Deficit Disorder, then clearing clutter is going to be difficult as ADD people lack the ability to concentrate on any one thing for long. These people hurl themselves into a job 100%, moving it into the sphere of compulsion, and then just as abruptly stop whatever job they are doing. Unfortunately, that compulsion usually goes into just one particular part of the clearing project, so a small part will be cleared, while the bigger picture remains unattended to.

Learning to finish what you start is important, especially if you want to move on in life and have people respect you, so pay attention to the finishing rather than the starting. Everyone finds the beginning part easy, and fun, but few finish what they start; which is why only a few make it to the top and why most new businesses fail.

Force yourself to be aware of everything and everyone around you. Stop thinking about what you want to say in a conversation and how to protect yourself from any negative comment, by giving others a chance to speak. See how dropping the armor from you could give you much more in the long run. After all, if the armor is constantly around you then others can't get close enough to help.

Try to bring more balance into your life by calming the mind with yoga, meditation, or taking a few minutes for yourself each day, away from everyone around you.

Learn to take more responsibility for your actions, responding less to criticism along the way.

Also read # 23 - The Overeater.

Fear of failure

Most of us know what failure is, because
most of us have failed at something at
some time in our lives. But fear of failure,
in this case, is the need to evade failure by
not starting, or finishing, anything. And
having a cluttered home is the perfect
excuse not to try: how can you become
a success if you can't clear enough space
to start anything?

The fear of failure is often connected to fear of success—
producing the same inaction --and most certainly comes
from seeing failure in the family and the effect it has on
family members. Witnessing a parent fail, whether at
sports, business or the arts, can leave an indelible mark on
a child who then believes that every member of the family
is doomed to fail at anything they try.

These clutterers are the dreamers who think "I could,"
rather than "I did." They feel "I could be as good as that"
but never start in order to prove it. The fear of others
judging them as a failure, instead of someone willing to
try, limits their opportunities in careers and in life as they
move back into the shadows, not forward into the light.

Fear of failure leads to inaction and often goes with being a perfectionist. If the quality of the work is unattainable, then there is little point in beginning!

Clutterers who fit into this category, have usually known many others who have failed, but instead of taking the time to analyze why the failure occurred—lack of money, of contacts, of the right ideas or products—they see failure as the ultimate destination, highlighting the difference between those who become successful after suffering through a failure, and those who can't see beyond it.

Failed people stop. Successful people keep going long after the failure, making the field of successful people smaller, and the degree of success much more attainable.

These people expect failure and when it arrives say, "See, I knew I'd fail" fulfilling their own prophesy. But failure is something that has to be learned. Toddlers don't know failure when starting to walk. Very young children don't know failure when painting. The difference between failure and success is that some people go down, while others go up, and the change in direction is usually linked to years of being beaten down by others and then by themselves. Those who choose to move up, however, are the ones who refuse to let others dictate the course of their lives.

People who fear failure usually present themselves as such, and their clutter collection is the excuse they need to remain a failure.

Also read #15—Being a Perfectionist, and #4—Fear of success.

Remedy

To get beyond the failure frame of mind, talk to others who have failed and then gone on to be a success at something. Then you'll know that one defeat isn't the end of the world.

Many successful people—including millionaires—have failed at many things in their lives before they finally found something to be a success at. Failure is part of success. It's the learning curve of defeat that gives you the information on how to become a winner. So stop procrastinating and making excuses and start to clear the clutter. See that as the first step towards a goal that you really want to achieve.

> ### SUGGESTION
>
> When you are about to give up on something, move beyond it and push through to the end, no matter what it is. Finish that pile of papers on your desk – before you leave work for the day. Be more assertive in your speech. Take small steps to become a success, then take bigger steps once you feel more secure.
>
> Feel the difference between when you feel like a failure and when you're successful at something.

Take a class in something that you were told as a child you were no good at—usually art or music. Do something that will bring you closer to seeing that failure is all in the mind—one persons failure can be another's success.

Many people have the same idea for a product at the same time, but only one will make their mark, leading the others to think that the successful person has stolen their idea. If you have many ideas for products, then act on one and see where it leads.

Stop comparing yourself to others. Yes, some kids have made fortunes by the age of 25, but millions more haven't, so move beyond that stifling image and decide that you will join the crowd of winners, no matter what your age.

If you do fail, then what? Is someone going to have to bail you out? Rally around? Is that what you're waiting for? Are you willing to spend the rest of your life saying "I coulda" instead of " I did?" And if you have kids, what life lessons are you passing along to them?

So, start with organizing the clutter. Put papers together, clear clothes another time. Sort the kitchen another day. Go room by room, or put groups of items together. Toss, donate, give to friends anything that isn't going to be part of your new successful life.

Sort all the papers and set up a filing system for the important ones. Buy a shredder for personal papers that are no longer needed.

If the clothes you own don't make you feel like a success when you wear them, move them out.

Place confidence building post-it-notes all over your home.

Start a life as someone who is already a success—even if failures still happen. Move beyond it. You are not connected to a rope that links you to your failed family, so cut the cord and move on.

Read biographies on famous people and see how many failures they had before success smiled on them. Use the Internet to find out how many times famous people received rejections: writers, actors, singers, sports figures, inventors, entrepreneurs.

Success is pushing through to better things. Failure is giving up before finding out how close to success you were!

26

Fear of having relationships

This affliction affects both males and females, and having a cluttered space is a great excuse not to invite people over and be social. Yet, many of them who put up barriers are also the ones who yearn to be married and have a family.

So what are they really afraid of? Being judged? Being intimate? Having their space invaded? Being naked?

Clutter and piles of papers, clothing and general mess, are barriers to success, relationships, interacting with others and being part of life.

These people want to get close to others, but fear that their lack of attractiveness will limit any connection to anyone looking for a real relationship. They limit themselves by what they deem to be attractive, rather than allowing others an opinion to the contrary.

They make the excuse of being too tired to make the effort, although really they just don't feel worthy or interesting enough.

Clutter for these people is a way of shutting out the world by making people pass the obstacle course to get in, thereby making it plain they are not interested in spending time with others, or, making it so difficult, that only those sincerely interested will make the effort. Fear of exposing themselves to the outside world keeps the clutter securely in place.

Many of them are couch potatoes, often overweight, but all with low esteem.

They dread being judged for things they say and do, or how they look. But often, fear of being judged is absorbed and learned from family who constantly put down a child for having an opinion that didn't match the prevailing one at home, or for just being different. Or, in some cases, they are seen as the overachiever in the family who is a success at work but not in their personal life, the one who can't find a husband/wife because they are too busy with their careers. And the family never lets them forget it.

These clutterers don't clear the mess even if they are highly organized by nature, using it as as their only excuse not to be social and to keep unsympathetic family members from entering their home.

Fear of intimacy can start at any time, unlike the other emotions which often start in childhood. It can start with cold, unemotional parents who never gave the skills of intimacy to a child desperately wanting closeness. It can start in puberty, in the teen years after a first difficult sexual experience; or even in marriage if the husband/wife is judgmental. Or it can be connected to religion, which may see intimacy as something dirty and for procreation only.

Whatever the reason, these people need tender, loving care and to know that they have value just for being who they are.

Remedy

It's difficult to become a parent if you don't have a relationship, so what are you most afraid of? Showing your body? Showing your emotions? Showing who you really are? Making a commitment to someone or something?

How did you grow up? Was your home life unhappy? Did you grow up in a home with anger or violence? Is the problem with you or what the home represented? Are you afraid of getting into the same situation as your parents? Afraid that whoever you get involved with will also be judgmental? Or, was intimacy seen as something to push away?

> **SUGGESTION**
>
> If you have paintings and photographs hanging on the walls of your space, what message are you sending out. Take a look around your home. Are they photographs and pictures of single people? If so, take them down and find pictures that have two people in them, or a family. If the pictures are of animals or birds, make sure they are a pair – or a family.

Know that you don't have to follow in your parents footsteps and that you do deserve to have a happy home life and a loving relationship.

Clear the clutter and feel how safe you feel in the space? Is there something missing?

Do you feel a sense of calm or unease? Try to pinpoint where the feeling comes from.

Is there too much open space that it makes you feel fearful?

Do you need a smaller apartment in order to feel safe? Is the space big enough for one or two people? Is it so small that only one person could live there? If so, that may be your objective—an unconscious decision to stop another from entering. Or, is the rent so good that you can't move, or don't think you can?

Invite people back to your cleaned-up place for drinks, coffee, or just to see it. Be proud of it. Make it a welcoming place. If you have an image problem, then work on that too.

If you want to be in an intimate relationship then make the bedroom a special place. Buy gorgeous sheets and a light that dims and gives off a glow. Often, the bedroom is the last place people spend time and money on, thinking the living space more important—which is it to many—but if you are looking for a loving relationship, then the bedroom should be one of your first priorities. Spray the room with scent. It doesn't matter if there is only you sleeping in it, make it sensual for you.

Buy sexy lingerie, and if you're a man, sexy underwear— yes, it does matter to women!

Buy a Feng Shui book and use the ideas. Put in more mirrors and candles and play music that makes you feel sexy.

As your sense of confidence begins to grow, so will your desire to move out into the world.

Clear up the kitchen and learn to cook. Food and sensuality go together, so learn to enjoy good food, even if you cook and eat alone. Learn about foods, which ones are more seductive than others, which ones have aphrodisiac powers. And if you don't usually drink wine, splurge on a bottle occasionally.

Clear a pathway through all the clutter and feel the difference. An opening up of your space, and yourself, will eventually pay dividends.

27

Everything is not valuable

Television shows such as "The Antique Road Show" are great, but they have also brought out the worst in many families. Now everyone thinks everything must be valuable and no one will part with anything.

And even though many of these clutterers know that some of their items are worthless, they've been so brainwashed by TV shows, eBay and other selling sites, that now nothing is allowed to leave their homes. If it will bring them money, even a tiny amount, they are willing to takes hours of their time selling the items.

But this isn't always about the money, as most people believe it to be. Sometimes it's just about winning, feeling that they got something in return, even if the hours spent selling, doesn't equate with the money they received. It's the feeling of impoverishment, needing to receive compensation for their own lack, for being undervalued.

Often believing themselves to be underrated at work, at home, and in everyday situations, they watch "The Antique Road Show" and make comments about the worth of their own possessions as compared to the ones on the show, needing to find something of value in their lives, some-where. These clutterers become pack rats in order to connect their personal worth to the worth of the object. If it is of value and they own it, then they too must be smart for having seen a good reselling price in it when they first bought it—even if no such idea entered their minds at that point. And the clutter mounts along with their expectations of making a killing.

This is also a hoarding mentality, the "can't let anything go" mind set. It's a feeling that everything must be saved, just in case it should suddenly—and miraculously—appreciate in price.

These clutterers expect that they will make money where others have failed, and if others have actually sold, then their object must surely be worth more. It's delusional thinking that stops them from being discerning as they clear and sort the real junk from items that may have some value.

To make an objective decision about the worth of their items, they often need help, but instead of seeking out the information from books, web sites, or vintage and antique sales, they'd rather keep the cluttered mess around, waiting for that one-in-a-million chance.

It is also greed, the fear of letting something go and then finding out later that they made a mistake. Lack of decision-making skills, lack of taking responsibility and fear of doing the wrong thing, all play their part in this clutterer's mind.

Remedy

It's the getting something back that's the stumbling block here.

Did everything in your childhood have a pay back. Did you have to give something to get something back—a hug in return for being told how wonderful you were? Did you have to give something in order to get gifts—make a fuss over an aunt to get a new toy?

Did your parents, or grandparents, instill in you that everything had a value? Did they have a poverty mentality left over from their childhood—or were they genuinely poverty- stricken?

> ### SUGGESTION
>
> Take an item that you think has value. Now find out what its real value is. Look on the Internet, look at books in bookstores and at the library. If you think it's really a valuable antique, take it to a reputable dealer and have it appraised. Do this with one item per week. Who knows? You may hit the jackpot, but if not, move the item on.

Everyone loves a bargain and everyone wants to buy something at a flea market for $1 that is really worth $10,000, but be realistic: how often does it happen?

If you genuinely have something that may be of value, then find out. But if you find it has very little value, give it away. How much time will it take to sell the item, versus how much is your time worth? Work out the hourly rate of selling something on an Internet site. How does it match up to your hourly rate as a worker? If the time isn't worth it, then donate the item and get a tax break.

If you have kids, let them help. Get them to do the legwork on the Internet and give them a cut if they can sell the item for a great price.

Go to the bookstores and look up to see if your object is valuable. Now that there's such an active market for antiques and collectibles, there are many books with pictures and prices in them, so check them out. But be warned, just because they list something for $200, it doesn't mean that you would get that amount for your similar-looking object. You have to find just the right market to give you a good price, and that often takes time.

Ask yourself why you hoard, why you need to get something back. Are you compensating for feeling undervalued, either at work or at home? Has a friend, family member or neighbor, made money selling on Internet sites? Do you feel envious and so now need to do the same?

Pick out the items you think are worth something and then get rid of the rest. Make piles, some for donating, some for friends, garbage bags for stuff to toss.

Fill the bag and take it over to the thrift store and feel good about donating—instead of being angry at the time spent on the Internet and in bookstores, only to find out that the item was worth just a few dollars.

Stop collecting, unless you really have a love for particular objects and know what you're doing.

The less you hang on to stuff, the more likely you are to get something good back into your life further down the road—even if you don't end up on "The Antique Road Show."

28

The kids are gone, but not their stuff!

It's one thing for kids to go off to college and leave most of their possessions behind, but many parents have been keeping things for their kids for years, even decades, and most of it isn't valuable—if it were, the offspring would have taken it way before this.

And most of the things that are stored for years and have little value, are tossed eventually, so why are parents the saps hanging onto them? Things that seemed so important after school and college are no longer important once kids grow up and get their own job, home, spouse and kids. But how many parents have moved not only their own belongings, to new homes, downsized apartments, or even storage spaces, but their sons'/daughters' stuff too?

These parents make excuses for their offspring not collecting their possessions long after they have their own places, turning the kids into less responsible adults and allowing them to become clutterers—even if the clutter is in someone else's home—and also turning their parents into clutterers by default.

Many have kept their kids' old school books for decades, only to see them tossed when they finally arrived home to go through their boxes—years after college ended.

But boxes are not the only things these parents keep for their brood; many parents keep their rooms just as they were when the kids left to go to college or to set up their own home. These are the parents who just can't let their children go, insisting that maybe their child will return at some point, or in an emergency situation. And that emergency is now happening more and more, as sons and daughters—in their twenties and thirties—return to the nest as a cheaper way to live.

But even though home should be a refuge, do parents really want their adult kids to come back into their lives?

Many of them now return to have lower rent, a house-keeper, cook and laundry maid. Someone to clean their rooms, prepare meals and clean up—and mothers are usually the ones to do it, although fathers are often the ones with the car keys, money and perks.

Some, use mom and dad's home to store winter/summer clothes for the change of seasons, while others see it as a place to store everything they just can't part with strollers, toys, baby clothes, furniture and much more.

Some parents are even willing to store furniture for their kids in the basement, spare room, even paid storage spaces.

The empty nest syndrome, for many parents, drives them to hang-on to their kids' stuff for as long as they can— before they finally realize that the kid(s) have really flown the nest. The final acceptance that they are now a couple, once again.

Remedy

Call up the kids and give them a time limit to take their stuff. Tell them you want their room for a guest bedroom, painting studio, sewing room, anything you like, but it's not a storage room for their possessions any more.

If you've done a good job bringing them up, they'll understand. If they don't, then what did you miss in their upbringing? Deadlines always push people into action so don't be afraid to use it for your brood.

Do you see holding their possessions as being their way back to you, some sort of hold over them, something that gives meaning to your importance and their need—even if it is only extra space for their worldly goods? If so, cut the cord. They have left the nest and now's the time to do the things that you want to do, in your space, and if that entails setting up a studio or office, then do it.

Why should you have to clutter your home with their collections making your home smaller in the bargain? Or, is there an ulterior motive? Do you have a marriage with little communication, so that keeping the kids' stuff stored forces them home sometimes in order to renew that past family life? Or, is your husband/wife complaining about storing their paraphernalia and you see it as a way of getting back at them, even winning over them?

Look at why you are keeping things that may have little use. Is it out of generosity, or something much deeper? Are you finding it difficult not having the kids around? Don't know how to fill you time? Feel depressed? If it is to bring the kids back, then you may be storing their stuff for the rest of your life.

If the kids can't make a decision on what to keep and what to toss, help them. You've probably been through it before, but don't be overly generous with your space—unless you have unlimited space and you don't care.

If they are on the move, either changing jobs or homes, and don't have a permanent place, then offer to rent a small storage space for them—but make them sort through everything before putting things into storage, otherwise, you may be paying for a storage space only to have the stuff tossed as worthless at a later date.

Most kids who are fresh out of college want to keep all their school books, but within a few years they'll be ready to let them go as new things come into their lives—like a family of their own.

Be firm with yourself, too, and ask if you're keeping their goods and chattels because of their need, or yours? And if you keep moving homes with their belongings in tow, when they have a place of their own, then shame on you!

The word FREE does not mean that YOU have to take it!

No matter what it is, these people just have to take free things. The word "free" has a magnet attached it, and these people have an antenna that works from a mile away. They pick up papers, other people's junk, leaflets, magazines, free makeup samples, anything that doesn't have a price tag to it.

They take all the free things offered in supermarkets and food stores. They enter competitions in the hope of getting something for nothing; never understanding that the information they give away is far more important to the business than the prize being paid out.

They take office supplies as a perk of the job and compensation for lack of a good paycheck, never understanding that their paycheck is based on the losses of the business. They will take anything offered to them regardless of whether or not they need it, want it, or know someone to pass it along to.

These are the people who are afraid of missing out, of missing the boat, of others having more than they have. It's the scarcity mentality, of taking it while it's there; otherwise, they'll be angry later on that they didn't take it when they had the option.

But taking everything also implies that they are not clear about their likes, dislikes and needs. Taking magazines and free literature home to read later is fine, if the papers are then recycled, but most people who take free stuff are not that discerning. They pickup newspapers that others have left behind, just in case they may need the information later. They take free pens, for future use; samples of anything and everything, to save money; free food samples, even if they dislike the food being offered.

They take other people's magazines from the recycle paper piles. Clothing from others, even if they don't really like the garment. Perfume samples even if they don't like the smell, makeup samples even if they don't like the colors. They read last week's newspaper just because it's there to read; old news be damned.

This is a question of restraint, priorities and need. Do they really need it, or are they unable to stop themselves? In childhood there may have been too many "no's." Or maybe there was a lack of "no." Or, parents who told them to take everything they could—before others got to it.

Ultimately, this is about not being able to say "no" to whatever is being offered.

And part of this is greed, part insecurity at missing out, and part lack of understanding why everything that has the word FREE attached to it is such a draw.

Remedy

You are the advertising people's dream. They know how addictive the word "free" can be and market it accordingly to people like you. But watching someone grab everything that's free is not a pleasant sight, signifying a feeling of lack and greed, all at the same time. Is this how you want to be seen?

A feeling of lack and short-age in your life, gives the impression that you think you can't make it on your own, and taking supplies from work sends the mes-sage to your coworkers, and yourself, that you feel less and so need to take more. It implies that you have to get yours—like the other workers doing the same thing—before whatever it is, runs out; that things are finite, that there isn't enough to go around.

SUGGESTION

If you go into a store and they are passing out free samples, walk on. No looking back, no circling around the counters and back again. No hesitation. Move forwards towards what you really want – to buy.

Try to stop yourself from taking free things. Make it a game you play with yourself.

The more you toss and organize your home, the less likely you will want to clutter it with free items and the leftovers of others.

And the office is not an extension of your home. Many people seem to think that the word "office" means stor-age space—free storage space—for all the stuff they don't want cluttering up their home. But clutter and personal items eventually cut into work time and the ability to focus, so take the things home, or purge them. And free office supplies actually cost YOU in your wages. All that extra expense goes against the office expenses, which lowers the profit line for the business; which ultimately means that you won't get that raise in wages that you've asked for.

Be selective. Wouldn't you rather be known as someone with good taste than as someone who can be bought with the word "free?" Make a decision that you will become more discerning. Think about all the ads for expensive things that aim for the customer with Discriminating Taste, the one who wants the best and doesn't want to follow the crowd.

Picking up everything because it's free means that you don't fit into that customer base, and if you want to move up in the world and be their customer, then pay your own way.

Go back to your childhood and see where the mind set comes from, then address it.

If you take the discarded clothes of others because they're being given away, break the habit—unless the clothes are fabulous and make you look fabulous. Cultivate your own image. What do you want to look like, smell like, be like? If you are not sure, then look at how others dress and follow that. But make sure it's a look that will bring you great responses, not derision. Go to stores and look at clothes to give you more ideas. Try them on.

What do you want your home to look like? What type of things do you want to decorate it with? Decide, and then move towards that decision. Decide who you want to be five years from now, and ask yourself if taking anything free is going to get you there. If not, put it down and leave it alone.

30

Kids and Their Rooms

Just because kids clutter, it does not mean they will grow up to become clutterers. Trust me! Most kids are clutterers because the world is new and filled with interesting things. It isn't until they get older that they whittle down the decisions, opportunities and "stuff." Kids haven't got that far yet, so adults need to be patient.

The problem for most parents is that what they consider junk, the kid(s) consider a treasure—and "treasures" for most parents equate with junk that can be tossed. But think about the things adults keep: old letters, playbills, film tickets that have meaning, hubcaps, license plates! So how bad is the kids' junk really? And where did they pick up the habit of making unimportant things seem so important?

Kids are creative—at least until the educational system gets to them—and so they need to have many things in their rooms that appeal to their active minds: meaning that they need systems they can see, much like creative adults.

And because kids have little control over their lives, their rooms become a place of refuge, a place of their own to do as they like, a place where adults rarely visit—or should visit.

Some kids are bigger clutterers than others and some kids have more interests, which if allowed to be pursued, will often carry on into their adult years to become a hobby or side business. So, enthusiasm for a variety of subjects should be seen in a positive light, not as adding more clutter to the already overcrowded room.

Problems often arise when parents see their kids as an extension of themselves; meaning that a mess in the kids' room equates with them being bad parents. And, as the parents imagine it, to the outside world also looks like an inability on their part to direct both the offspring and the clutter.

For some parents the mess is also seen as control, and that control, taken by a child who refuses to clear up a messy room, is something they are unwilling to let happen as it then undermines, so they think, their authority.

But messy kids often grow up to become curious adults with creative and interesting jobs in the arts or sciences, so parents need to discern if the mess is creative and important, or just a child/teenager testing the parent.

And only the parent is really the one to judge that.

Also read #9 --Being Creative.

Remedy

Apart from having a no food rule—good for critters, bad for the household—for kids' rooms, don't sweat it. It isn't worth it. Close the door, and from time to time throw in clean sheets, checking that the dirty ones come out. Give them a time limit to change the sheets, and if they are old enough, make them do their own laundry. They'll appreciate it when they get to college—and their future husbands/wives certainly will.

Help them to clear their rooms by making it an afternoon event. Bring up snacks and drinks, for clearing time only, and line the hallway with boxes. On one side of the hallway place boxes for donations, the other side for projects and things they want to keep. Divide the boxes up and label them. Do it for the entire family and make it fun, not a chore. Order pizza and make it a day-long experience if an afternoon isn't long enough. Then go out for a treat in the evening—dinner, ice cream or a walk, something out of the ordinary which signifies that a good job was done by all.

> ## SUGGESTION
>
> Instead of nagging the kids to clear up, give them plenty of containers—plastic if possible — to put their treasures, projects and "stuff" into. If you have the space, give them bookshelves for their books and a table to do their school work and projects on. Twice a year, clear out what they don't want or need—no excuses!

Give each kid a "maybe box"—don't we all change our minds about items we think we can part with—but make it no bigger than a wine box. Give them a time limit for the maybe box, three weeks perhaps, giving them a chance to take back any item they'd rather not part with, but after the time limit has ended, donate, toss, give away. And make sure that YOU follow through with it so that the kids know that you mean business.

Trying to keep kids' rooms under control is usually a losing battle, so quit the nagging. But never bribe your kids to clear up, either, as you will set them up for a lifetime of payoffs—even in relationships. Better to let them make the decision to want to clear the clutter: at some point it will get beyond even their tolerance point!

Appeal to their higher nature, their wanting to do good by donating out worn toys and sports equipment. Recycle rather than toss. Get the kids into a healthy lifestyle rather than one based on bribes, bartering and nagging.

And never throw anything away without their permission—it is still their stuff, not yours.

Do the kids have enough places to put their clothes, toys, games? If not, acquire something additional: cheap, found, or a container you already have somewhere else in the home. Help the kids along. Kids need to see things, so give them lots of plastic containers that will show what's inside.

Don't spend time fighting the mess, it's usually just a phase, and if it isn't, then help creativity along. Many messy children have grown into famous, creative adults, able to give their parents all the good things that money can buy.

Now, wouldn't that be a nice tradeoff!

31

I'm moving

Searching for the perfect place to live, these people wander the world. They bounce around from one home to another, one city to another, one country to another.

They are the transients of the world.

Usually single or divorced, and having left numerous relationships behind, these clutterers are not settled in their minds and are pining for a stable relationship, home and job, in order for them to feel secure. What they end up with is a constant hopping from place to place, relationship to relationship and job to job, leaving the security they crave unattainable. They don't have stability in relationships or anything else in their lives, because the first thing out of their mouths when they meet someone, is that they will be moving on. They are already looking for another place to live, another job, relationship, or whatever else they think they need to move on to. Everything they say points to their being on the way to somewhere else, leaving them with a lack of understanding about why they can't achieve a happy life.

These clutterers usually have plenty of options of where

to move to next, and are of the mind set that if they move to that place, they will, finally, be fulfilled. They live in a delusional way, always thinking the grass is greener on the other side, and constantly waiting to find it. Filled with self doubt, they are always finding fault with whoever they are with or wherever they are, which leads to lives filled with anger and frustration.

This type of individual is usually running away from an unhappy childhood where the home was anything but welcoming. Verbal or other abuse is often part of the problem, but instead of trying to understand why they feel the need to keep moving, they just keep hoping that a spouse, child, stable relationship, job or home will bring them everything they are looking for. Never do they think to turn inwards to find the answers, always outwards towards their next move.

Clutter, for them, is something to clear and sort only when they are ready to move on to a different location, whether it is another house/apartment, city, state or country. It is not a job to bother with in order to make their space more comfortable and inviting, either for themselves or others. They have so little self esteem and so little belief in their abilities, that a wonderful home, so they think, could only be achieved by someone new coming into their life to give it to them.

These are clutterers who feel they don't deserve a great place to live and will camp out wherever a place is offered; usually taking the least appealing option. They don't understand that they could have a real place to live if only they were at peace with themselves.

Remedy

Go back to the way you grew up, and where. What was it that made you want to run away? Parents who argued, or who didn't communicate? Siblings who made home life unbearable? Words that cut deep? An abusive household?

Or, are you adopted? Many children who are adopted— even by loving couples— find themselves adrift in the world, without understanding why. If you know you're adopted, and have never made the effort to find your real mother or father, would finding them make you feel more settled, or, would the truth make you feel less stable?

> ## SUGGESTION
>
> Imagine that the place you are now living in is to be your last home. How do you feel about that? Horrified? If so, then seek out a better living arrangement and make that place into a real home. Buy fresh flowers or objects that you really like. Take an interest in how the space looks and feels. Invite others into it.

Why are you so dissatisfied with life and yourself? What are you really craving? Take a good hard look at who you are now. Listen to the words you say, actions you do, thoughts you have. What do you look like? Do you take care with your appearance? If not, how do you present yourself to the world? If you don't care, why should the world respond in a positive way to you?

Why give you a better job if you have a negative attitude to it as soon as you walk through the door? Why have a great place to live, if you can't keep it clean and neat?

Why would anyone want to come into your life, if you are

moving on? Do you think you deserve to meet someone special, or do you just dream of it happening?

In short, the problem and the solution are not out there; they are inside yourself. And if you are not willing to do the work to understand why you need to constantly stay in motion, then the merry-go-round will just keep on going, and going, with you going with it, becoming more and more unhappy and dissatisfied with life as you go around.

Pick a place you feel you'd be happy living in, and then hunt for a job in that area. If you envy others, see what it is about them that you envy. If it is something you can emulate—like dress or having a more likable personality— then work on that.

Often, being unhappy and dissatisfied come from health problems and not taking care of the situation. If you are depressed, then seek help, but also make sure that you are eating good, nutritionally balanced foods. Find a better place to live that will give you a kitchen to cook in, and then take an interest in food. Experiment with things you wouldn't normally eat. Be more adventurous.

Join a gym and exercise—which will immediately make you feel better—and make the effort to meet more people. Take a class in something you enjoy, that will connect you to like minded people. And make it a rule never to tell anyone that you will be moving soon. Be more optimistic about putting down roots.

Once you feel more settled, then others will want to connect to you. After all, it's difficult to hit the bull's eye if the target keeps moving.

Too much stuff. Really?

It's difficult to imagine anyone thinking
they have clutter when they don't, but
some people actually do think this. It's a
compulsion fueled by the mind-chatter
going around and around their heads.

This mind set is akin to people being on the move. They are
not content in their homes, don't feel at home there, and
are constantly trying to find ways to make home, become
a home. But to them, there is always something missing.

Usually their homes are cold and uninviting, even though
they constantly move furniture around, redecorate, buy
new drapes and anything else they imagine the place needs;
never understanding that the unhappiness isn't due to the
home, but is due to the life of the person who thinks it's a
cluttered place.

These people can never get their possessions down to the
few they actually think they want. They donate, toss, refur-
bish, clear out, but still it never satisfies them. The lack of
satisfaction is within themselves and usually they are trying
to convince themselves that all is well, when it isn't. They
buy, panic and then toss. Buy, panic and then toss. It's a
treadmill that just keeps going and going.

Many of these people overachieve in everything they do. They were good in school, college, at their jobs. They look good and they take care of their appearance, but nothing is ever good enough. They could remove much of everything they own from their homes and they would still think they had too much stuff. It's like being an anorexic, only with homes instead of bodies, and it represents the same attitude.

Moving beyond this is difficult as they want perfection, and in their minds it would be attainable—if they could just downsize enough.

It's a compulsion, like constantly washing the hands, and these are compulsive people who want their husbands/wives to be just right, their children to be just right, their homes to be just right, and themselves, especially, to be just right.

They never feel that they are perfect enough for their spouse or parents, or any other family member. They live by the book and still beat themselves up.

It is a deep psychological problem that needs addressing professionally in order to understand where the feeling that nothing is ever good enough, comes from.

Remedy

Ask yourself why you constantly feel overwhelmed and what is driving you out of the home—not into it. What is the underlying problem? Is it a bad marriage, a stifling marriage or lifestyle? Are you locked into something you feel you can't get out of? Do you want to change jobs, go to a new city, country? Break out? Is the house too big, the responsibility too great? Are you trying to achieve perfection, when perfection doesn't exist?

Work through all the reasons you don't feel at ease in your home, and then do something about it. If you are a perfectionist, understand that there is no such thing as perfection as it's a moving target. As soon as you reach it, it moves. Give it up and accept that good is good enough. Your best, is all that's required. The home doesn't have to be perfect.

If you live with someone else, work through who they are and what you think they expect from you. Are you trying to live up to their expectations, and if so, why? If the situation in your home is making you unhappy, sit down and talk about it. Go to a marriage counselor if talking with your husband/wife is too difficult. And if all else fails, move out for a while, or leave the relationship. If you stay in the relationship, and are a parent, then it may make you ill, or even harm the children, so take some action.

SUGGESTION

Practice the art of letting go. Learn the difference between what a real home looks like and what a showcase home looks like. Homes are for living in, not places to feel intimidated.

Let a little mess appear, and if you do start to panic that you have too much stuff, then sit down, close your eyes, and tell yourself that you deserve to have a home that you love—and be damned with perfection!

Is your partner a neat-freak and you are afraid of not coming up to their standards? Or, maybe the expectations are really yours, not theirs. Did you grow up in a perfect home, or one that you were ashamed of?

Are you trying to keep up with a sibling who has the perfect home? Did you grow up in a family where you were expected to excel—in every direction? Are you a non-working parent when you'd rather be working? Do you feel undervalued at home, but valued at work? Are you trying to compensate for that feeling of being undervalued in the home, by trying to run a perfect household?

Were you the hope of the family, the one everyone had high expectations of?

Were you the perfect child while your siblings had all the fun? Are you still trying to live up to the expectations of others, especially the in-laws and other family members?

Go through all the reasons for having this fixation to downsize everything in your home.

Home should be a place to relax in and enjoy, so make yours a happy, welcoming space, not only for guests, but especially for yourself. Leave a little mess and see how it feels. Don't jump up to clear the dishes after every meal, and let the kids leave some toys around. Relax more and see what the family response is? And start to live your life for yourself, not them.

Also read # 15—Being a Perfectionist

33

Noise clutter

The TV is on, the headphones are on, the computer is on; a way of filling their heads with as much noise as possible. Clutter not only surrounds these people, but their heads are cluttered too, and when the music and noise stop, they start—to talk, talk, talk. They talk on the phone, talk through the computer, talk to anyone who will listen. These people fear silence. Silence for them represents a space to fill so that reality cannot enter.

They live in their own little world and fill it day in and day out. They store tangible stuff as much as they stuff their heads with noise, and their homes are usually indicative of their state of emotional turmoil.

Often labeled as having Attention Deficit Disorder, these clutterers take the label willingly as an excuse for their mess, not only in their homes but also in their lives; lives that have little direction. What most of these people really are, is fearful. People trying to balance their existence but with little understanding of how to balance anything, from checkbooks to time, as they retreat behind a wall of noise.

A little like the crisis maker, they are usually dependent on others, to listen, loan them money or to pull them out of a jam.

When this overload leads to depression, which it usually does as the problems compound, they find themselves unable to move forwards, allowing family and friends to then label them as a failure, someone who just can't "get it together," forcing them to retreat behind an even higher wall of noise.

As the mind-chatter grows, so the inability to concentrate on anything for long, also grows. They can get so bogged down on one particular action that they waste time doing unimportant things. They can clean an oven for a couple of hours, instead of wiping it down in three minutes, but find paying bills an impossible task.

As they retreat further and further into the wall of sound, technology becomes their security blanket, a way of reaching out to others, but without the responsibility of having to be there physically. A dependancy on technology that would leave them with withdrawal symptoms—much like a drug addict—if the noise was taken away.

Anything connected to time, is a problem for these individuals, and unable to get anywhere by an appointed hour, they sabotage their future by pushing themselves further away from the things they most want in life. They pride themselves on the fact that they can multitask, when in reality each task is never quite finished, or is finished in an unsatisfactory way—the noise in their heads taking over from the real chore at hand.

Remedy

The only way forward is to bite the bullet and turn off all the noise: the TV, the computer and the phone. Force yourself to turn off the noise for at least 30 minutes a day until you feel comfortable with the silence. Try to remember what in your childhood made you want to drown out the other noises. If the words from your parents or school were cruel, how did you respond? Did you retreat into your own world, a world that was safe and secure?

If so, now is the time to come back into the real world.

Ask yourself why you can't let silence enter your life. Did you grow up with a lot of noise? Did your parents argue a lot and the noise drowned that out? Did you have loud siblings?

Were you a bad students and noise drowned out the teacher's comments?

> ### SUGGESTION
> Force yourself to sit in silence each day for a few minutes – no excuses. Learn meditation techniques to help you dissolve the mind-chatter. If you live in a noisy, crowded city, find one place to call your own where you can sit quietly. There are many nooks and crannies in buildings and parks.
> Seek them out.

Find out where the fear of silence comes from, or where the need to have constant noise comes from.

Take a long shower or bath—in silence. Sink into the silence and feel how wonderful it feels to have no one and nothing creating a noise in your head. Take a walk in the park. Learn meditation and yoga.

If you can, take a trip to the ocean, a lake or mountain, then force yourself to sit there without earphones, cell phone or a computer. Learn to separate from the computer and the chatter it produces.

Train yourself to finish what you start. This is especially important if you're trying to impress on people at work that you are responsible. Show them that you can see things through to the end if given the chance.

Make lists, lists, lists—something all ADD people protest they cannot do. All excuses of course, all excuses that send the message that you don't want to have to grow up and take responsibility for your actions.

If you don't take charge over all the noise in your head—real noise or mind-chatter—it will stop you from getting the jobs you really want and from the kind of life you really want to be living, producing even more chatter to what is already going around and around.

It will also stop you from having rewarding relationships and friendships, as others walk away from you and the impenetrable wall of sound.

So, cut the cord on all the noise and learn to be more discerning; and how much better you can function. And remember, successful people do—as in action; unsuccessful people fill their lives with unnecessary people, noises and actions.

Also read #14 --Lack of Time. #17—Crisis maker, and #18—Not taking responsibility

About the Author

Thea Maii is a painter, costume and clothing designer who has worked in professional theater and television in the US and England. Since 2004, she's been helping individuals and businesses become clutter-free through her organizing business - Tame the Space. She's a reformed clutterer and lives in Manhattan.

More at www.tamethespace.com

Made in the USA
Charleston, SC
18 March 2012